# What Your Colleagues Are S

As a new kindergarten teacher, I found myself being totally overwhelmed with teaching my students how to write. Let's just face the facts—our kiddos come to us not knowing how to hold a pencil, and they are expected to leave knowing how to write a story with a beginning, middle, and end. I had such a hard time understanding how to get from point A to point B . . . until I was introduced to these amazing nursery rhyme prompts and writing structures. It changed everything!

The nursery rhymes are such a fun and easy way to build those writing skills for little ones. My class loves the nursery rhymes that we read before the writing activity—and I love it too, because it is an easy way to build those text-to-self connections in a meaningful way. We usually complete one section of the writing structure each day, and build on it throughout the week. Then, we revise and rewrite for the final copy. I love the results every time. Another great thing about these writing activities is that they are often easy to connect to other pieces of literature that are used in the classroom. For instance, I read the book *Harold B. Wigglebottom Learns About Bullying* by Howard Binkow to my kiddos, and we used one of the nursery rhyme activities as a reading response! It turned out so well!

—**Kathryn Gibson,** Kindergarten Teacher,
Conroe Independent School District, TX

I was thrilled to use the nursery rhyme writing tools in my gifted and talented program. From kindergarten to fifth grade, the structures allowed students to see that writing is not as hard as they had once thought! You could visibly see the excitement rise as they explored, created, imagined, and composed their very own writing samples—and it was *fun!* They began asking to do more, to go deeper, to create more complex ideas, and as we continued using these tools, their writing abilities grew from basic skills to more intricate and elaborate compositions. Thank you for these resources!

—**Julie Brawner,** K–5 Teacher,
Oak Creek Elementary,
Comal Independent School District,
New Braunfels, TX

Finally, a resource that helps teachers build critical oral language foundations with nursery rhymes while teaching young students to practice writing with the same predictable language structures. The reciprocal power of this approach with classic rhymes is a game changer!

—**Nicole Morales,** Literacy Coach,
Ed White Elementary School,
Clear Creek Independent School District,
Houston, TX

# TEXT STRUCTURES From NURSERY RHYMES

For all the primary teachers who have longed for a little more help with teaching writing.

# TEXT STRUCTURES From NURSERY RHYMES

Teaching Reading & Writing to Young Children

**50+ Rhyme and Lesson Pairs**

## Gretchen Bernabei
## Kayla Shook
## Jayne Hover

With Illustrations by **Andrea Cotham**

**resources.corwin.com/nurseryrhymes**

CL CORWIN LITERACY

FOR INFORMATION:

Corwin
A SAGE Company
2455 Teller Road
Thousand Oaks, California 91320
(800) 233-9936
www.corwin.com

SAGE Publications Ltd.
1 Oliver's Yard
55 City Road
London EC1Y 1SP
United Kingdom

SAGE Publications India Pvt. Ltd.
B 1/I 1 Mohan Cooperative Industrial Area
Mathura Road, New Delhi 110 044
India

SAGE Publications Asia-Pacific Pte. Ltd.
3 Church Street
#10-04 Samsung Hub
Singapore 049483

Publisher and Senior Program Director: Lisa Luedeke
Editorial Development Manager: Julie Nemer
Editorial Assistant: Nicole Shade
Production Editor: Melanie Birdsall
Copy Editor: Deanna Noga
Typesetter: C&M Digitals (P) Ltd.
Proofreader: Sally Jaskold
Cover and Interior Designer: Gail Buschman
Marketing Manager: Rebecca Eaton

Illustrations by Andrea Cotham

Printed in the United States of America

ISBN 978-1-5063-8796-3

This book is printed on acid-free paper.

Certified Chain of Custody
Promoting Sustainable Forestry
www.sfiprogram.org
SFI-01268
SFI label applies to text stock

17 18 19 20 21 10 9 8 7 6 5 4 3 2 1

# Contents

**Note:** *In this book, the lessons are organized alphabetically, according to the title of the associated nursery rhyme.*

Bale bale chocdate

Visit the companion website at
**resources.corwin.com/nurseryrhymes**
for downloadable paper dolls,
text structures, templates, and other resources.

# Acknowledgments

For piloting our lessons and sharing their insights and student work, we owe deep gratitude to the following teachers and school leaders: from Sippel Elementary, Lisa Newman, Lenore Sassman, Serena Georges-Penny, Julie Olson, Nancy Schlather, Shannon String, Connie Hernandez, Lori Kolodziejski, Andrea Vukela, Sunnye Krug, Kelley Leeds, Michelle Oliver, Laura Kunz, Mandi Roper, and Michelle Myles; from Thousand Oaks Elementary, Greta Hurley; from Stahl Elementary, Angie Mullinix; from Blanco Elementary, Kristen Schultz, Mindy Lay, and Jowie Walker; from Oak Creek Elementary, Heather Mizell and Julie Brawner; from Luling Primary School, Kathryn Gibson.

We owe special thanks to Paul Erickson from Brookhaven Elementary and Malley Johnson from Mary Lou Fisher Elementary School.

For her enthusiasm, encouragement, and organizational skills, we salute, embrace, and adore Judi Reimer.

Thank you to our Lisa Luedeke, brilliant and dear, for believing in our work, knowing our hearts, and understanding our lives. And thank you to the rest of our Corwin team: Julie Nemer, Nicole Shade, Melanie Birdsall, Deanna Noga, and Gail Buschman, and to Rebecca Eaton for your wisdom, both the practical and the whimsical.

From Jayne: Thank you, Jim, for encouraging me and cheering me on. You are not just an amazing husband, you are a precious gift to me. I thank God every morning that I get to wake up beside you.

From Kayla: Thank you, Paul, for being Super Dad while I worked long, late hours pursuing my dream of being an author. Thank you, Rory, for helping me understand how nursery rhymes help kids like you and for inspiring me to be the best.

From Gretchen: Thank you Julian and Matilde ahead of me, and Granny Williams, Nene, Sissie, and Aunt Ray behind me.

Finally, we feel grateful to those who came before us and created the nursery rhymes from which the youngest of our students can become confident writers.

# Introduction

## How This Book Began

Over the last 20 years, in the hundreds of teacher training sessions we've conducted throughout the country we've heard one unanswered wish from the teachers of the youngest grades: What have you got for us? Could you make some lessons for kindergarten? For pre-k? What about first graders?

We three talked with each other about how we had seen kindergarten teachers adapt parts of our work for their students, often using our graphic icons and adding more drawings.

Then, I watched Kayla teaching some of the simplest text structures and kernel essays to teachers of second graders. I thought about the text structures we had gleaned from pieces in American History for our secondary students and wondered what kinds of texts would provide structures that would feel natural to our youngest kids. And when Jayne explained to me about four- and five-year-olds' developmental need for rhythm and rhyme, the idea magically crystallized: We could extract the text structures from nursery rhymes! And so we did.

We realized, though, that seeing written, boxed-up text structures wouldn't do a thing for children who don't read yet, so we converted the text structures to illustrations to match both the text structures and the nursery rhymes. We found a brilliant artist in Andrea Cotham, who was able to convert the text structures into simple and charming line drawings. Now we had text structures in two forms: words and pictures. That way, students who read the drawings would begin to develop the habits of visualizing a text progress from one chunk to the next, before they read a single word!

Next, we sent the lessons out to classrooms, to teachers ready to try them out. We asked them to see what worked best for them. They reacted and enthusiastically returned to us an impressive variety of both student samples and teaching sequences. We also taught the lessons to children, and we visited classrooms to observe, to see for ourselves the impact of these lessons. If you teach young children, you will see the pleasure that we witnessed as children play with these nursery rhymes, both chanting them and using them to tell their own experiences.

Finally, we decided to add one more element to the lessons: the paper dolls. There are any number of ways to use these concrete tools for both reading and writing, and we offer a beginning set of ideas. The paper dolls are designed to be cut out, laminated, and pasted onto popsicle sticks for classroom use. To access the downloadable dolls and related teaching tips, visit the companion website at **resources.corwin.com/ nurseryrhymes.**

## How the Lessons Work

Here is what you will find for each lesson.

Each lesson has two pages. The writing lesson page is on the left side.

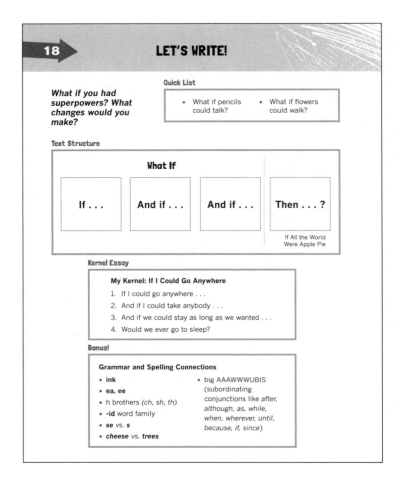

On this page, you will find the following:

- The text structure, written in boxes with words

- A "quick list" to jumpstart a conversation with your students about topics they may have, topics that will work well with that text structure

- A sample "kernel essay," which demonstrates the process of combining an original topic with the text structure

- A grammar/conventions connection, listing language arts points you can find in the nursery rhyme, for handy extension

The reading lesson page is on the right.

On this page, you will find

- one nursery rhyme;

- the same text structure as on the writing page, but with illustrations instead of words; and

- large font for the beginning of each step in the text structure. These are helpful when using pointers, which you can use to signal when to look to the next picture. This will assist children with learning to track left to right.

We suggest using these lessons with the purpose of developing independent writers. Here are some basic teaching steps:

1. Each lesson should begin with a reading of the nursery rhyme and a discussion of the plot. Young students do not need in-depth teaching on each of the structures of the rhyme, but they do need exposure to academic vocabulary. Simply referring to the **plot** and the **characters** of the rhyme exposes young readers and writers to these terms. After reading the rhyme, you may wish to continue reading it as a choral reading, talk about words that rhyme, or show the text structure along with the reading.

2. After the rhyme is read and the plot discussed, you may choose to wait until the following day to continue with a writing activity. We suggest spending 1 to 2 weeks on each rhyme.

3. Once the text structure is introduced, we suggest writing a class version. In pre-k and kindergarten, this may be the extent of the writing activity for each rhyme.

4. If students are ready, the next step is for students in small groups to create their own version.

5. When students are confident enough, they move on to independent work or work with a buddy.

You will notice text structures with different numbers of boxes. It might be helpful to begin with the rhymes that use three boxes, because these have a simpler structure. There is no particular order for going through these lessons. In fact, it might be beneficial to take advantage of an everyday experience and then find a structure that matches. For example, after a holiday weekend, Ms. Johnson used "Bye, Baby Bunting" and the text structure "Where did they go?" She knew her students had just said goodbye to many visiting grandparents and family members who gathered over the weekend. The structure gave the children the opportunity to say things like "My grandmother went home. She gave me a new blanket. I wish she would come back."

A few more examples of typical classroom experiences and useful text structures might include:

| | |
|---|---|
| a guest speaker in the classroom | Polite Q and A (Mary, Mary, Quite Contrary) |
| a rained-out event | A Disappointment (Old Mother Hubbard) |
| someone went on a trip | Small Talk (Pussycat, Pussycat) |
| someone loses something | I Lost Something! (Lucy Lockett) |
| someone got hurt | Ouch! That Hurt! (Jack and Jill) |

We know pre-k and kindergarten students do not necessarily tell stories in order, and these structures help develop that skill. To support the development of younger students, these lessons provide the structure in pictures first, then labeling, adult transcription, and finally independent student writing. As students acquire writing competencies in Grades 1 and 2, you can skip steps like transcription and "reading" the picture structures, using the word structures instead and independent writing. You will find various template pages to use throughout this process. Differentiate by choosing the processes and templates that work best for your individual students.

This book makes use of nursery rhymes to teach patterns and structures of writing. As you travel through this book, you will see familiar rhymes from your childhood and some not so familiar. You will notice we are using rhymes from English-speaking countries only. Rhymes from other countries do not translate with rhyme and rhythm, which makes them not useful for our purposes.

To enhance the process, we have also included language arts extensions such as grammar suggestions. Example: You might teach -ck following short vowels when looking at Jack Be Nimble.

As students create whole class, small group, and individual versions of the rhymes, they are assembling their own nursery rhyme book. As you experience these text structures with your students, consider helping them create their own book to share with their family.

The following are student examples from various age groups, using various kinds of stationery. Some show the nursery rhyme converted to kernel essays; some show original drawings and teacher transcriptions; some show original writing that follows the text structure; some student work follows a different drummer. The point isn't so much that they follow the structure of the nursery rhyme as it is to give students a scaffold to create a story that has *a* structure.

Two teachers shared their detailed methods.

## Paul Erickson's Pre-K Classroom

Paul began by gathering his pre-k class to the carpet, where they read the nursery rhyme three ways. First he read, then they echo-read, then they all read together.

There was an Old Woman

There was an old woman who lived in a shoe
She had so many children she didn't know what to do!
So she gave them some broth without any bread,
And she whipped them all soundly, and put them to bed.

Next, he worked on the first part of the text structure (in this case, the first line).

He flipped to the next page on the chart tablet, where he had already written the line. "Now, what do you picture? What does that look like to you?"

Students raised their hands and answered what shoes they visualized, what they thought the old woman looked like, and he drew their ideas.

He did this on a separate page for each part of the nursery rhyme.

"How many children do you think she had?" Paul solicited ideas for the drawings, and the children watched their contributions become part of the drawings.

"She had no bread . . . okay. What do you think broth is?"

By the time they got to the last chunk of text, the students had become very familiar with the text and with the practice of drawing their thinking. It was fun!

After this process, he brought out the text structure on a new sheet of paper and the children worked through it together, creating their own (group) composition.

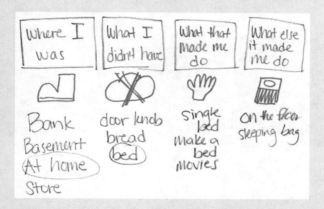

"Let's see . . . where might I have been?" Students brainstormed "The bank!" "The basement" "At home!" Paul wrote them all down. Together, they selected (and circled) one, then went to the next step and repeated the process.

By the time he finished all four squares, the group had created a story.

After this, he allowed the children to take a clipboard and draw their own stories.

They drew, then showing him their drawings, told all about the drawing.

He recorded them to post digitally for parents to access. Several of his students' pieces are featured in this book.

Later, he would redraw a cleaned-up copy of the group composition. These were all around his room from previous days.

*(Continued)*

(Continued)

Paul created this graphic to show his process, starting with the "Read the Nursery Rhyme" step.

## Nursery Rhyme Essays

**Students Write**

The students will draw a picture relating to their personal experience with the prompt. The students will dictate responses. As the year progresses, the students will begin to label and write words and phrases.

**Teacher and Students Edit the Draft**

The teacher will read the draft to the students, then will read it again and pause during certain points to add elements to the story. The teacher will ask students to add more visual details (five senses), story elements (mostly beginning and end), or personal feelings to the draft.

**Teacher Writes**

The teacher takes the parts of the brainstorming and puts them together into one writing piece.

**Read the Nursery Rhyme**

**Read the poem four times.**
1. I read, you listen.
2. I read, you echo.
3. We read together.

During the fourth read, the teacher will read the poem line by line. After reading each line, the teacher will prompt the students to describe what the teacher should draw to help visualize the line. The teacher will draw the pictures.

**Brainstorm Using Kernel Essay**

**Read the first section of the frame.** Have the students brainstorm ideas that fit the prompt. The teacher will write the ideas on the chart. The teacher will select one of the ideas to continue with to the next frame.

**Read the next section.** Tell the students that they are going to focus on just the idea that was selected in the previous section. Have the students brainstorm ideas for the next section. **Repeat with the rest of the sections.**

## From Malley Johnson, Kindergarten–Grade 2

Here is how I taught each lesson to the kids at different grade levels.

1.  First, we read the nursery rhyme for enjoyment. We then did some choral reading and/or shared reading. We looked for things such as rhyming words, sight words, capital letters, and so on.

2.  Then we went through each line that aligned with the text structure. We discussed vocabulary and what each line meant. The kids shared what they thought it meant, either through visualizing it or discussion. Then we illustrated each part. We did this for each part of the text structure.

    As we discussed, I made sure to use the same words used in the text structure, so when we were ready to write, they were prepared. For example, for "To Market, to Market," *first I bought _____, next I bought _____, last I bought _____.*

*(Continued)*

(Continued)

3. Next, we looked at the text structure. We discussed what we could write about, what item we could make, and three ingredients needed to make it. Once we agreed on a topic, we went through each stage of the text structure and formed our sentences together. We even did our illustrations together.

4. Students then were given a chance to think about their own topic. Then they turned and shared with their partner. They did this with each part of the text structure. Thought about it, paired up, and shared their ideas.

5. Then they wrote!

I think for the first time ever there wasn't a single student who said, "I don't know what to write about!" The structure was so laid out for them and ideas so simple to share and discuss. It still blows me away.

## Solutions to Writing Problems in the Early Grades

### Problem 1: Nonverbal Children

We know it's difficult to teach writing to children who aren't very verbal, those who are mostly quiet. Talking is a great solution. Use the nursery rhymes, reading them aloud, pointing at words with puppets, pretending the puppets are reading. Giving the children practice in the oral texts of nursery rhymes enriches their text inventory, while using rhyme and rhythm and teaching the patterns and fun of language.

### Problem 2: Canned Writing Programs

Another problem is finding a balance between too-prescribed teaching and too-unstructured workshop time. Canned programs leave teachers feeling handcuffed, and the students are not engaged; yet teachers need some guidance. This set of lessons provides a solution, giving teachers plenty of concrete steps, with loads of flexibility.

### Problem 3: Students Learn to Hate Writing as Soon as It's Academic

We don't think there is enough transition between fun "pretend" writing and academic writing. This book bridges that gap. Following a structure is absolutely academic, but it has all the fun of pretending, of whimsical rhymes, of rich out-loud sharing.

## Quotes From Our Hall of Fame Writing Theorists

Since these favorites of ours led us to create this book, we would like to share a few of their guiding thoughts.

### Mem Fox

There's Mem Fox (2008), who teaches us that reading should be enjoyable. A snuggly, warm, singing kind of young experience. Further, she teaches us the importance of rhythm and rhyme for children.

> Experts in literacy and child development have discovered that if children know eight nursery rhymes by heart by the time they're four years old, they're usually among the best readers by the time they're eight. (p. 89)

And just what do students gain?

> Once children have masses of rhythmic gems like these in their heads, they'll have a huge store of information to bring to the task of learning to read, a nice fat bank of language—words, phrases, structures, and grammar. The words in their heads then begin to drift into their daily speech, and all at once we have an articulate child. (p. 93)

### Donald Graves

Canned writing programs are not the answer. Donald Graves suggests that teachers who only have one day a week for writing should not teach writing at all. "You will encourage poor habits in your students and they will only learn to dislike writing" (Newkirk, 2009). Creating a classroom with fertile conditions is the way, where students have daily time and lots of choices. In fact, the three "pillars of writing instruction," according to Graves, are "choice, time and response" (Newkirk, 2009, p. 175). All three can be built into these lessons—and should be.

### Lev Vygotsky

Some people think that play serves the purpose of recreation, but for young children play provides a much wider background for changes in needs and consciousness. "Action in the imaginative sphere, in an imaginary situation, the creation of voluntary intentions, and the formation of real-life plans and volitional motives—all appear in play and make it the highest level of preschool development. The child **moves forward** essentially through play activity" (Vygotsky, p. 102).

In imaginative play, a child "reads" a play environment and "composes" within it. "Creating an imaginary situation can be regarded as a means of developing abstract thought" (Vygotsky, p. 103).

In play, a "new relation is created between the field of meaning and the visual field—that is, between situations in thought and real situations" (Vygotsky, p. 104). This leads to another remarkable thought about the importance of play: A child voluntarily submits to a system of rules, even as "rules of pretend." This is something that Vygotsky regards as an important marker in the child's development of will, of consciousness, and later, of morals.

As a child matures, the play continues. The child starts to skip steps, skipping the "acting it out" part and the playacting becomes internal, known as imagination. A "what if" becomes part of this process.

In writing, that "what if" becomes a part of the writing process. Remembering is a kind of pretending, and inventing the future is pretending, too.

With the introduction of right or wrong answers, or right or wrong writing, all play comes to a halt, and the only "what ifs" are anxiety-filled and not growth-producing. They can result in the groan coming from students when it is "writing time."

### John Hattie

When we see the impact of our teaching actions, we can tell how we are doing. John Hattie summarizes his remarkable syntheses of voluminous research in a talk, leaving the most powerful challenge to teachers: to use what he calls the Kenny Rogers Theory of Learning.

"The most impactful teachers are those who continually and effectively and collectively evaluate their impact on students" (Hattie, 2017). This will lead to knowing when to hold 'em and when to fold 'em.

### James Moffett

The only way to know when to do anything with students is by paying attention to them and, in the words of the educational titan James Moffett (1987), "heeding better the feedback we get about the consequences of our own teaching actions" (p. 210).

\* \* \*

Some teachers start with the nursery rhymes.

Some teachers start with students' experience.

Some end up with nursery rhymes the students know by heart.

Some end up with group-written original pieces.

Some end up with student-written original pieces.

Some end up using the structures to write about a different story.

Some end up with student drawings and conversations about the drawings.

As Thomas Newkirk tells us, "Teaching is profoundly situational." And so teachers may use whatever parts, whatever sequence they find useful for their own students on any particular day.

We hope you enjoy reminiscing with us through these wonderful nursery rhymes and that you create your own memories with your students.

## References

Fox, M. (2008). *Reading magic: Why reading aloud to our children will change their lives forever*. Orlando, FL: Harcourt.

Hattie, J. (2017). *It takes a teacher: A talk by John Hattie*. Retrieved from https://educationonair .withgoogle.com/live/2016-dec/watch/keynote-au.

Moffett, J. (1987). *Teaching the universe of discourse*. Portsmouth, NH: Boynton/Cook.

Newkirk, T. (2009). *Holding on to good ideas in a time of bad ones: Six literacy principles worth fighting for*. Portsmouth, NH: Heinemann.

Vygotsky, L. S. (1978). *Mind in society: The development of higher psychological processes*. Cambridge, MA: Harvard University Press.

# Lessons

# LET'S WRITE!

*Think about something unusual that may have happened at school or at home.*

**Quick List**

- The fire truck came to school
- A lost tooth
- New family member
- A visit to a nurse or dentist

**Text Structure**

## Not What I Thought Would Happen

| How surprised I am | What you used to do | What you do now |
|---|---|---|

A Diller, a Dollar

**Kernel Essay**

**My Kernel: Sequoia Moved!**

1. I can't believe it.
2. You used to come over every day.
3. Now you live in California and you don't come over after school.

**Bonus!**

**Grammar and Spelling Connections**

- used to
- questions
- compound sentences

## A Diller, a Dollar

**A** diller, a dollar, a ten o'clock scholar,

What makes you come so soon?

**Y**ou used to come at ten o'clock,

**A**nd now you come at noon.

# STUDENT KERNEL

## Not What I Thought Would Happen

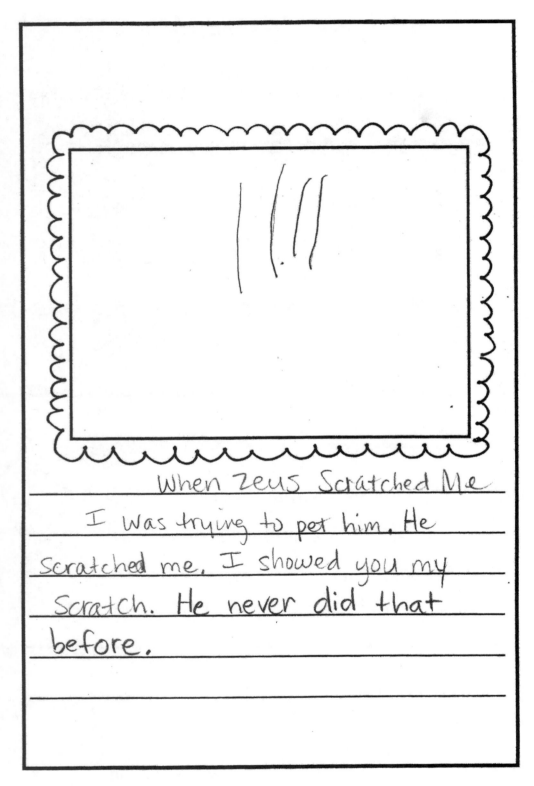

When Zeus Scratched Me
I was trying to pet him. He
Scratched me, I showed you my
Scratch. He never did that
before.

Olivia Keyes, Prekindergarten

# STUDENT KERNEL

## Not What I Thought Would Happen

**My Topic:** eDiting

| 1 How surprised I am | 2 What you used to do | 3 What you do now |
|---|---|---|
| I'm very surprised. | I ate vegetables. | Now I eat chips. |

Rory Shook, Kindergarten

**My Topic:** I used to have a tee

| 1 How surprised I am | 2 What you used to do | 3 What you do now |
|---|---|---|
| I used a tee last year. | I had a tee ball stand. | Now the coach pitches to me. |

Connor McCorkle, Grade 1

# LET'S WRITE!

***Think about someone you have seen who you recognized—someone "famous," even locally.***

## Quick List

- Seeing Ronald McDonald
- Spotting their teacher at the grocery store
- Seeing someone surprising on TV
- The Cat in the Hat visited the school
- A veteran visited the school

## Text Structure

### Spotting Someone Famous

| Where I was | Who I saw | What I thought |
|:-----------:|:---------:|:--------------:|

As I Was Going by Charing Cross

## Kernel Essay

**My Kernel: Seeing Snow White**

1. I was walking around Disneyland.
2. I saw Snow White!
3. She was beautiful.

## Bonus!

**Grammar and Spelling Connections**

- proper nouns
- **ar, or, ir, ur** (Charing, horse, first, burst)
- **ea** sounds (dear, heart, ready)
- AAAWWWUBIS
- exclamations
- ba-da-bing
- four colors

## Glossary

**AAAWWWUBIS\*:** subordinating conjunctions like *after, although, as, while, when, wherever, until, because, if, since*

**ba-da-bing\*:** a sentence containing three parts: *what your feet were doing, what your eye saw, and what you thought*

**four colors\*\*:** color coding a text to show talking (pink), seeing (blue), doing (green), and thinking (yellow)

**pitchforking\*:** embedding lists in writing

\*For more information, see *Grammar Keepers* by Gretchen Bernabei (Corwin, 2015).

\*\*For more information, see *Fun-Size Academic Writing for Serious Learning* by Gretchen Bernabei and Judi Reimer (Corwin, 2013).

**NURSERY RHYME**

## As I Was Going by Charing Cross

**A**s I was going by Charing Cross,

**I** saw a black man upon a black horse.

They told me it was King Charles the First,

**O**h dear! My heart was ready to burst!

# STUDENT KERNEL
## Spotting Someone Famous

My Topic: A tree with no bark

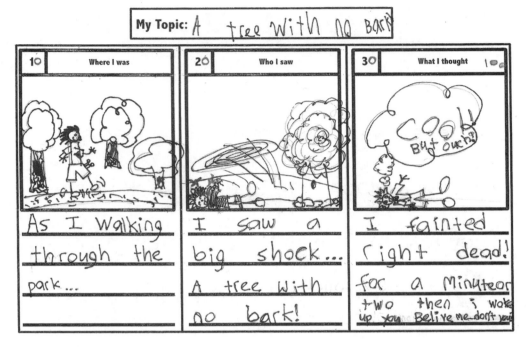

| 10 Where I was | 20 Who I saw | 30 What I thought |
|---|---|---|
| As I walking through the park... | I saw a big shock... A tree with no bark! | I fainted right dead! for a Minuteor two then i woke up you Belive me...dont you |

Willard Schultz, Grade 2

My Topic: Kitty

| 1 Where I was | 2 Who I saw | 3 What I thought |
|---|---|---|
| I was walking down the street | when I Saw a sweet Kitty sitting in the light | And I thought it was the cutest sight. |

Christine Flores, Grade 2

# STUDENT KERNEL
## Spotting Someone Famous

My Topic: Seeing Brohomers

| 1 Where I was | 2 Who I saw | 3 What I thought |
|---|---|---|
| As I wes shopping through the store | I saw Brohomers looking For more | I stood there and thought I would hit the door. |

Jackson House, Grade 2

My Topic: LeBron

| 1 Where I was | 2 Who I saw | 3 What I thought |
|---|---|---|
| As I was walking through the Park. | I saw leBron dashing in the Dark | and I thought I Was one lucky lark. |

Brooklyn Rhodes, Grade 2

*Think about how everyone has more than one of some things.*

## Quick List

- Toys
- Games
- Shoes
- Snacks
- Rocks
- Collections

## Text Structure

### More Than One

| | | |
|---|---|---|
| **Question: Do you have _____?** | **Answer: Yes, I have _____.** | **List them.** |

Baa, Baa, Black Sheep

## Kernel Essay

**My Kernel: Stuffed Animals**

1. Do you have stuffed animals?
2. Yes, I have stuffed animals.
3. I have a pink bunny, four mice, one dolphin, and two fluffy puppies.

## Bonus!

**Grammar and Spelling Connections**

- alliteration
- question/answer
- **ull/ool** *(full, wool)*
- pitchforking (embedding lists in writing)
- commas in a series

# Baa, Baa, Black Sheep

**B**aa, baa, black sheep, have you any wool?

**Y**es sir, yes sir, three bags full!

**O**ne for the master, one for the dame,

And one for the little boy

Who lives down the lane.

# STUDENT KERNEL
## More Than One

Austin Lea, Prekindergarten

Kruz Znidarsic, Kindergarten

# STUDENT KERNEL
## More Than One

My Topic: Willard

| 1 | Do you have ____? | 2 | Yes I have ____. | 3 | List them. |

Willard Willard do you have any Pok'emon cards.

Yes Jackson Yes Jackson i have a dox full or them.

some for brooklyn and som for me and some for calvin ant that maks three!

Jackson Lecce, Grade 2

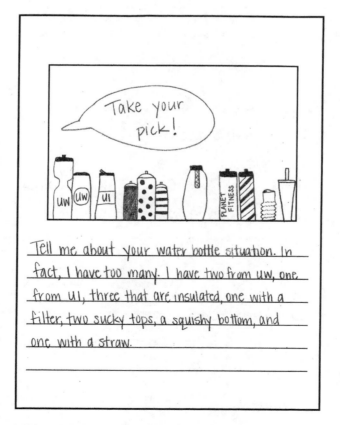

Take your pick!

Tell me about your water bottle situation. In fact, I have too many. I have two from uw, one from ui, three that are insulated, one with a filter, two sucky tops, a squishy bottom, and one with a straw.

Miranda Million, Teacher

# LET'S WRITE!

***Think about something you used to have—something you don't have anymore.***

### Quick List

| | |
|---|---|
| • Lost blankets | • Outgrown shoes |

### Text Structure

**Something I Used to Have**

| What I used to have | What happened to it | How it ended |
|---|---|---|

Betty Pringle

### Kernel Essay

**My Kernel: Skates**

1. I had some skates.
2. One day they were too little for me.
3. Now I don't have them anymore.

### Bonus!

**Grammar and Spelling Connections**

| | |
|---|---|
| • y to i | • contractions |
| • **-ig** (*pig, big*) | • commas in a series |

## Betty Pringle

**B**etty Pringle, she had a pig,

Not too little and not very big,

When he lived, he lived in clover,

**B**ut now he's dead, and that's all over.

Billy Pringle lay down and cried,

Betty Pringle lay down and died;

**S**o that's the end of one, two, and three:

Betty, Billy, poor piggie.

# STUDENT KERNEL
## Something I Used to Have

Lincoln Smith, Grade 3

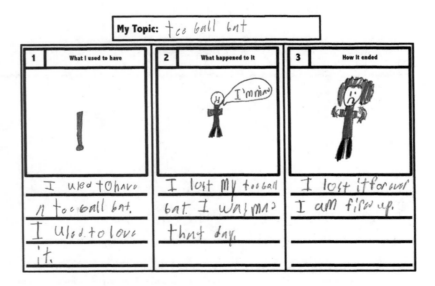

Connor McCorkle, Grade 1

# STUDENT KERNEL
## Something I Used to Have

**My Topic:** Panda

| 1 What I used to have | 2 What happened to it | 3 How it ended |
|---|---|---|
| When I was 6 I had a Panda Bear. He went with me every-where. | As the years went by he fell apart. It broke my heart. | Some one special heard about my Panda. and bought me a new one. |

Jim Hover, Author's Husband

# LET'S WRITE!

***Think about a time you've said goodbye and what you hope for when that person comes back.***

## Quick List

- Saying goodbye to the teacher on the last day of school
- Saying goodbye to your pet when you leave in the morning

## Text Structure

### Someone Left

| Somebody went away | What they looked like | What I want them to do |
|---|---|---|

Bobby Shaftoe

## Kernel Essay

**My Kernel: My Sister**

1. My sister went to college.
2. She was driving a red Jeep.
3. I want her to come home and play with me.

## Bonus!

**Grammar and Spelling Connections**

- contractions
- **ea, e, ee, y**
- plural (no apostrophe) vs. contractions (*Shaftoe's*)

## Bobby Shaftoe

**B**obby Shaftoe's gone to sea,

**S**ilver buckles at his knee;

**H**e'll come back and marry me—

Pretty Bobby Shaftoe!

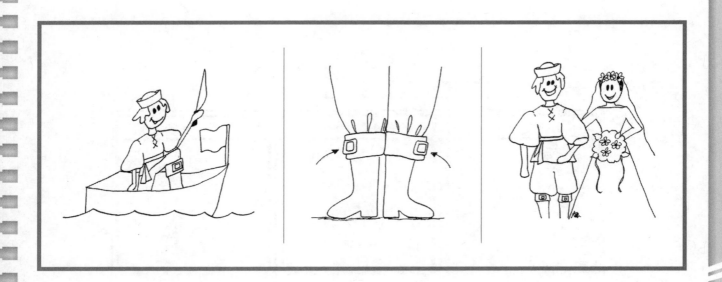

# STUDENT KERNEL
## Someone Left

**My Topic:** my Dog

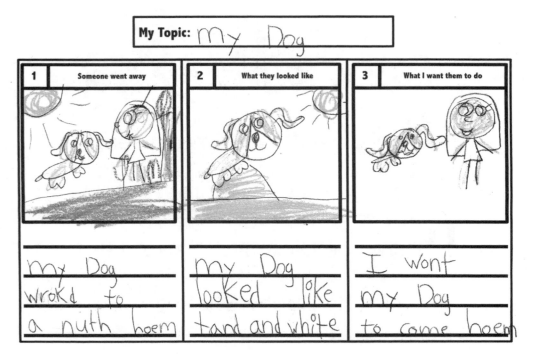

| 1 Someone went away | 2 What they looked like | 3 What I want them to do |
|---|---|---|
| my Dog wrokd to a nuth hoem | my Dog looked like tand and white | I wont my Dog to come hoem |

Victoria Hernandez, Kindergarten

**My Topic:** cycussin

| 1 Someone went away | 2 What they looked like | 3 What I want them to do |
|---|---|---|
| my cycussin wint away | thre look like thiss thae have brown her | I want them to cam bac |

Alorah Rodriguez, Kindergarten

# STUDENT KERNEL
## Someone Left

My Topic: mYdad

| 1 Someone went away | 2 What they looked like | 3 What I want them to do |
|---|---|---|
| MY dad went to atR | hey haR bRown hiR | I wot to gin me and misison a pisix |

Hunter Waite, Kindergarten

My Topic: my dvadm

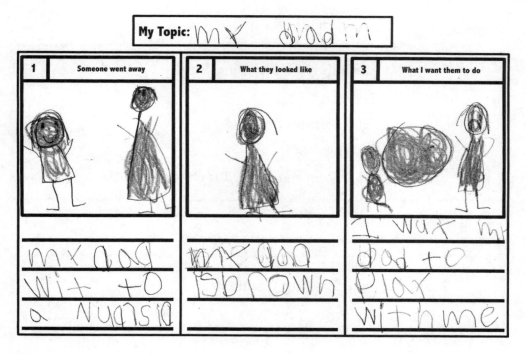

| 1 Someone went away | 2 What they looked like | 3 What I want them to do |
|---|---|---|
| mx and wit to a Nuansia | mx dad is brown | I wax m dad to PlaY withme |

Serenity Kelly, Kindergarten

# LET'S WRITE!

*Think about when you have news to tell at school!*

## Quick List

- You got a new couch or a new TV at home
- Someone got married
- Someone had a baby

## Text Structure

### Big News!

| You'll never believe this. | I've got news! | You'll never believe this. | The news is . . . |
|---|---|---|---|

Brave News Is Come to Town

## Kernel Essay

**My Kernel: New Sleeping Bag!**

1. Guess what!
2. I got something new!
3. Guess what it is!
4. It's a sleeping bag with Barney on it!

## Bonus!

**Grammar and Spelling Connections**

- repetition (*Brave news*)
- y to i
- adjectives
- name with apostrophe

# Brave News Is Come to Town

**B**rave news is come to town;

   **B**rave news is carried;

**B**rave news is come to town,

   **J**emmy Dawson's married.

# STUDENT KERNEL
## Big News!

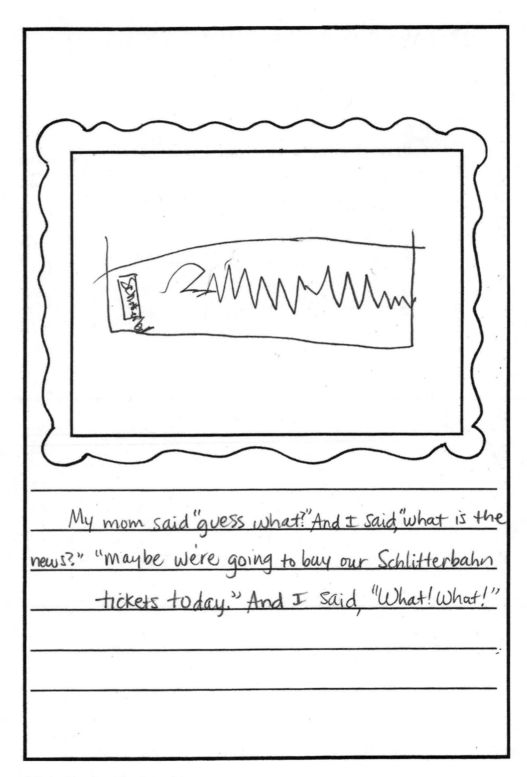

My mom said "guess what?" And I said, "what is the news?" "maybe we're going to buy our Schlitterbahn tickets today." And I said, "What! What!"

Olivia Keyes, Kindergarten

# STUDENT KERNEL
## Big News!

**My Topic:** Stephen Curry cams

**1** You'll never believe this

I got some news.

**2** I've got news!

Stephen curry came.

**3** You'll never believe this

the warriors came to town.

**4** The news is...

Oh my god Stephen curry came.

Connor McCorkle, Grade 1

**Think about when someone left to get something for you.**

## Quick List

- Someone shopped for your birthday
- Someone rented a movie for you
- Someone went to the store to get you some medicine
- Someone went to go get you some donuts

## Text Structure

### Where Did They Go?

| Bye | Where someone went | Why they went there |
|---|---|---|

Bye, Baby Bunting

## Kernel Essay

**My Kernel: Strawberries**

1. Bye, Mom!
2. Mom went to the store.
3. She went to buy some strawberries.

## Bonus!

**Grammar and Spelling Connections**

- **-ing**
- **-in**
- proper nouns
- alliteration
- **wr**

## Bye, Baby Bunting

**B**ye, baby Bunting

**D**addy's gone a-hunting,

**G**one to get a rabbit skin

To wrap the baby Bunting in.

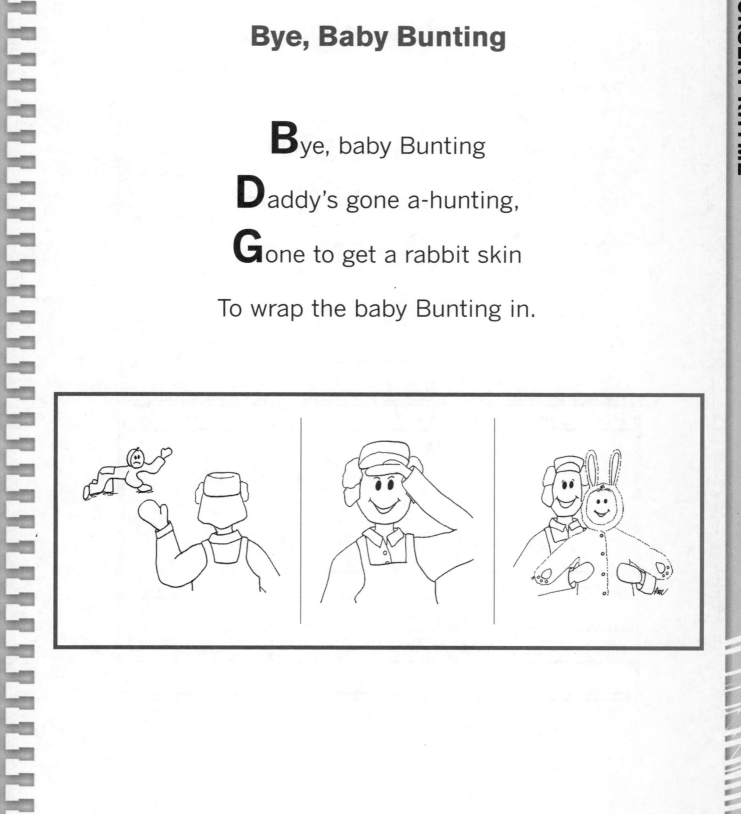

# STUDENT KERNEL
## Where Did They Go?

Jim Hover, Author's Husband

**My Topic:** Colorado

Jim Hover, Author's Husband

# STUDENT KERNEL
## Where Did They Go?

Connor McCorkle, Grade 1

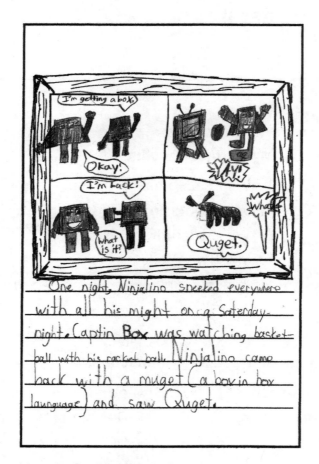

Lincoln Smith, Grade 3

**Think about a time you needed something you didn't have.**

## Quick List

- Ice
- Allergy medicine
- Glue
- Bread
- Gasoline

## Text Structure

### We Don't Have What We Need—Problem/Solution

| What we are missing (and need) | What we will do if we don't get it | We got what we need! | Yay! |
| --- | --- | --- | --- |

Cock a Doodle Do

## Kernel Essay

**My Kernel: Gasoline**

1. We needed gas in the car.
2. We might run out of gas!
3. We made it to a gas station!
4. Yay!! Yesssss!

## Bonus!

### Grammar and Spelling Connections

- onomatopoeia
- contractions
- short i
- **oo, o, oe** (ew sounds)
- **ou**
- **-ing** suffix/word part
- four sentence types

## Cock a Doodle Do

**C**ock a doodle do! My dame has lost her shoe.

My master's lost his fiddling stick and knows
not what to do.

Cock a doodle do! What is my dame to do?

**T**ill master's found his fiddling stick she'll
dance without her shoe.

**C**ock a doodle do! My dame has found her shoe,

And master's found his fiddling stick,

**S**ing cock a doodle do!

# STUDENT KERNEL

## We Don't Have What We Need—Problem/Solution

**My Topic:** Sleep

**1 What we are missing (and need)**

I need more Sleep!

**2 What we will do if we don't get it**

If I don't get more Sleep I may turn into a zombie!

**3 We got what we need**

My bed is calling my name.

**4 Yay!**

When I get sleep, I feel refreshed for my family.

Sarah Keyes, Mom and Nurse

# STUDENT KERNEL

## We Don't Have What We Need—Problem/Solution

**My Topic:** Eating Pudding

**1 What we are missing (and need)**

I tried to eat my pudding but didn't have a spoon.

**2 What we will do if we don't get it**

I can try to sip it with a straw but it's too thick.

**3 We got what we need!**

I found a spoon in the kitchen.

**4 Yay!**

My pudding was yummy.

Ruby Lacey Smith, Mom

# LET'S WRITE!

*Think about a time when you did something and explain how you did it.*

**Quick List**

- Kicked the ball
- Went to a birthday party
- Made an art project
- Baked cookies
- Rode a bike

**Text Structure**

## Something Happened

| What happened | How it happened |

Fiddle-De-Dee

**Kernel Essay**

**My Kernel: A Spinner**

1. I made a spinner.
2. I got a ball bearing and glued coins to it.

**Bonus!**

**Grammar and Spelling Connections**

- hyphens
- **ee, ied, e**
- y and y to i
- compound sentences
- **le**

# Fiddle-De-Dee

**F**iddle-de-dee, fiddle-de-dee,

The fly has married the bumble-bee.

**T**hey went to church, and married was she,

The fly has married the bumble-bee.

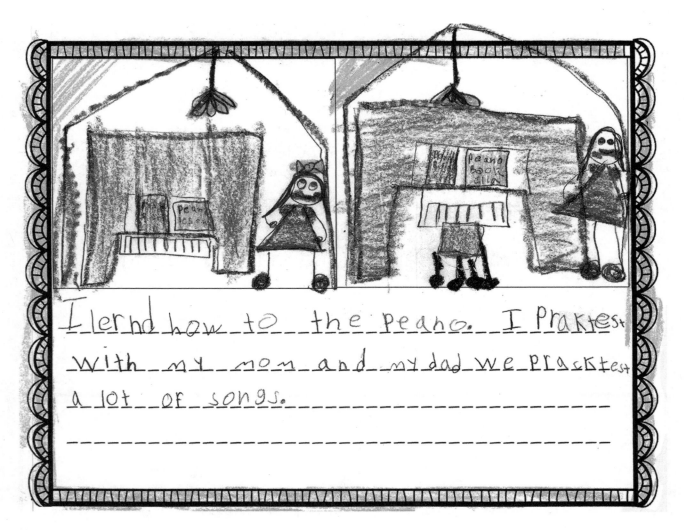

I lernd how to the peano. I praktest with my mom and my dad we praktest a lot of songs.

Ella Dominguez, Grade 1

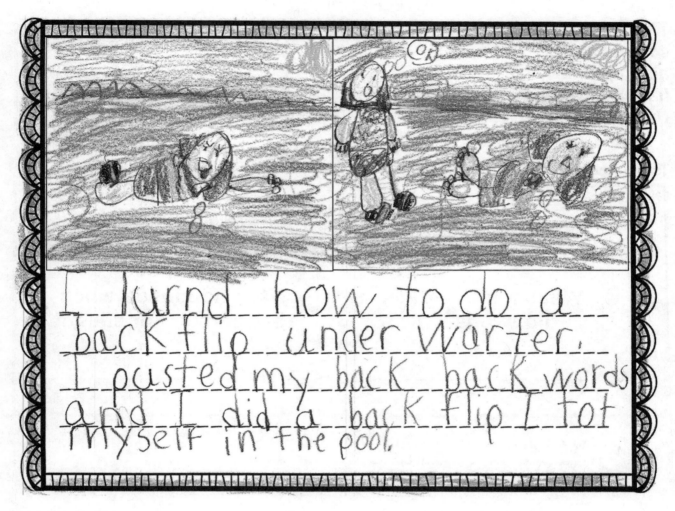

I lurnd how to do a backflip under warter. I pusted my back back words and I did a back flip I tot myself in the pool.

Analiese Franklin, Grade 1

# LET'S WRITE!

*Think about someone who acts up and what happens when they get caught.*

**Quick List**

- Someone broke a rule at school
- Someone was mean to someone else
- Someone called someone a name

**Text Structure**

## Getting Caught

| What someone did wrong | What happened when that person got caught |

Georgie Porgie

**Kernel Essay**

**My Kernel: The Stolen Snacks**

1. My friend ate some snacks without permission.
2. When his mom found out, he got grounded.

**Bonus!**

**Grammar and Spelling Connections**

- AAAWWWUBIS (subordinating conjunctions like *after, although, as, while, when, wherever, until, because, if, since*)
- plural
- alliteration
- **i** (*cry, pie*)
- **a** (ay, a_e)

## Georgie Porgie

Georgie Porgie, pudding and pie,

**K**issed the girls and made them cry.

When the boys came out to play,

**G**eorgie Porgie ran away.

# STUDENT KERNEL
## Getting Caught

| 1 | What someone did wrong | 2 | What happened when that person got caught |

He took his hat.

He will say sorry.

William Monge, Kindergarten

# STUDENT KERNEL
## Getting Caught

Matthew Cubit, Kindergarten

Valeria Santamaria, Kindergarten

*Think about having some free time and choosing lots of places to go. Where would you go first, next, last?*

**Quick List**

- A park
- A playground
- The fair
- A game room
- Any new place with lots to do

**Text Structure**

**Travel Map**

| Where should I go? | First . . . | Second . . . | Third . . . |

Goosey Goosey Gander

**Kernel Essay**

**My Kernel: On the Farm**

1. Where would I go on a farm?
2. First I would go to the barn to see the horses.
3. Then I would go to the pond.
4. Then I would ride on a tractor to the hay field.

**Bonus!**

**Grammar and Spelling Connections**

- question/answer
- possessives
- compound words
- rhyme patterns
- cvc (consonant-vowel-consonant) words

## Goosey Goosey Gander

Goosey goosey gander,

**W**hither shall I wander?

**U**pstairs, **d**ownstairs,

**A**nd in my lady's chamber;

There I met an old man

That would not say his prayers,

I took him by the left leg

And threw him down the stairs.

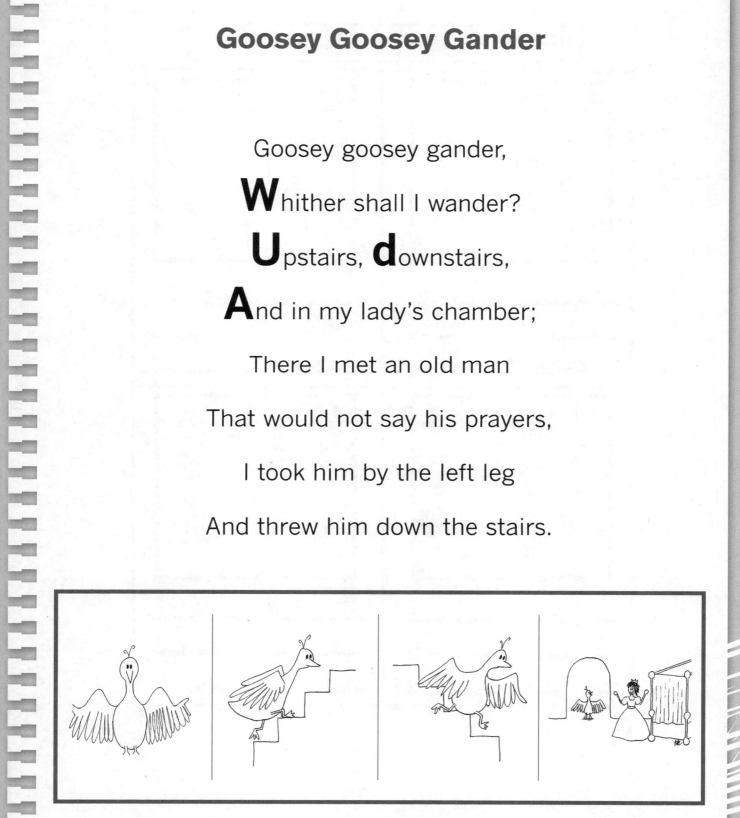

# STUDENT KERNEL
## Travel Map

**My Topic:** Eastes egg hunt

| 1 | Where should I go? |
|---|---|

I am going to a Eastes egg hunt.

| 2 | First... |
|---|---|

get redy and get my basckit.

| 3 | Second... |
|---|---|

wait and tell I get thar and wait fou thay get redy

| 4 | Third... |
|---|---|

I got a lot of egg.

Jimena Ramirez, Grade 2

# STUDENT KERNEL
## Travel Map

**My Topic:** my brothi's Phone

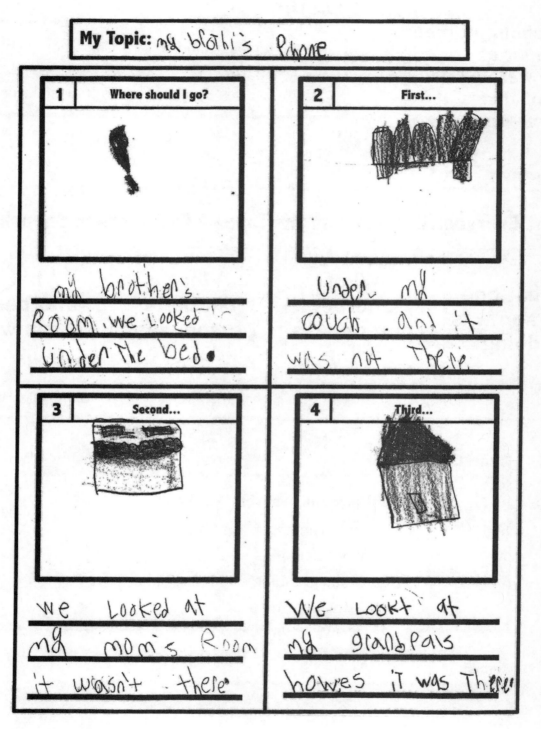

**1 Where should I go?**

my brother's Room. we Looked under the bed.

**2 First...**

under my couch. and it was not there.

**3 Second...**

we Looked at my mom's Room it wasn't there.

**4 Third...**

We Lookt at my granbPals howes it was There

Audrey Todd, Grade 2

# LET'S WRITE!

*Think about a time when a lot of people were all doing different things at the same time.*

**Quick List**

- On a playground
- At a party
- Classroom center rotations
- In the cafeteria

**Text Structure**

### What Everyone Was Doing at the Time—A Four-Person Snapshot

| What one person was doing | What another person was doing | What another person was doing | What another person was doing |
|---|---|---|---|

Hey Diddle Diddle

**Kernel Essay**

**My Kernel: Julian's Nerf War Party**

1. Will was running to his home base.
2. Noah was aiming.
3. Sam was grabbing more nerf bullets.
4. Alex was keeping score.

**Bonus!**

**Grammar and Spelling Connections**

- **le**
- past tense (**-ed** vs. *ran*)
- **oo**
- *cvc* (consonant-vowel-consonant) words
- **sp** blend

## Hey Diddle Diddle

**H**ey diddle diddle

The cat and the fiddle,

**T**he cow jumped over the moon;

**T**he little dog laughed to see such sport

**A**nd the dish ran away with the spoon.

# STUDENT KERNEL

## What Everyone Was Doing at the Time—
## A Four-Person Snapshot

**My Topic:** The dance

**1** what one person was doing

Some people were dancing in the gym.

**2** what one person was doing right then

Some were eating popcorn

**3** what another person was doing right then

Some were getting glow sticks.

**4** what another person was doing at that time.

I was wating for my friend.

Lily Keyes, Grade 3

# STUDENT KERNEL

## What Everyone Was Doing at the Time— A Four-Person Snapshot

**My Topic:** My favorite Music

**1  What one person was doing**

George was playing a guitar.

**2  What another person was doing**

Ringo was playing the drums.

**3  What another person was doing**

Paul was playing the bass guitar

**4  What another person was doing**

John was singing my favorite song. (Here comes The Sun)

Jim Hover, Author's Husband

# LET'S WRITE!

***Think about noises you've heard that made you jump.***

**Quick List**

- A fire alarm
- A siren
- Thunder
- Night noises

**Text Structure**

**Jump Scare**

| **What you were doing** | **A scary noise** | **What you did** |
|---|---|---|

Hickory Dickory Dock

**Kernel Essay**

**My Kernel: The Car Alarm**

1. I was going to sleep.
2. This loud noise started!
3. I ran to my mom's room and she said it was the neighbor's car alarm. It stopped.

**Bonus!**

**Grammar and Spelling Connections**

- alliteration
- past tense
- **ck**

## Hickory Dickory Dock

**H**ickory dickory dock.

The mouse ran up the clock.

**T**he clock struck one,

**T**he mouse ran down,

Hickory, dickory, dock.

# Hickory Dickory Dock

| What you were doing | A scary noise | What you did |
|---|---|---|
| sleeping [bed] -Addison | thunder | I covered up in my blankets |
| Sleeping [bed] -Karter | Growling in | I asked my mom what the noise was and she said it was the dog. |
| Playing with my toys in the Playroom -conor | thump thump | My mom said it was the engine on my Dad's truck |
| Playing Princess in my room -Sophia | a roaring noise | I told my brother to stop. |

Julie Olson, Teacher

# STUDENT KERNEL
## Jump Scare

I was walking to my trampaleh.
I herd a gun shote Boom Boom.
I skreamd and ran and hid onder my hed.

Ella Dominguez, Grade 1

I was doing my work. The
fire alarm went off. Then I linde
up and ran outside.

Andrew Burgon, Grade 1

# LET'S WRITE!

**Think about things your pet does.**

**Quick List**

- Ways it plays
- How it eats
- Where it follows you
- How it does tricks

**Text Structure**

## What My Pet Might Do

| My pet does this | Sometimes it's this way | Sometimes it's that way |
|---|---|---|

Higglety Pigglety

**Kernel Essay**

**My Kernel: My Cat Dottie**

1. Dottie America has rides in a baby stroller.
2. Sometimes I dress her up in doll clothes.
3. Sometimes she just wears her fur.

**Bonus!**

**Grammar and Spelling Connections**

- short vowels
- **ie**
- compound words
- repetition
- number words

## Higglety Pigglety

**H**igglety Pigglety, my black hen,

She lays eggs for gentlemen;

**S**ometimes nine and **S**ometimes ten,

Higglety Pigglety, my black hen!

## What My Pet Might Do

Chato kicking a soccer ball.
Chato sleeping on the porch.

Lily Keyes, Grade 3

# STUDENT KERNEL
## What My Pet Might Do

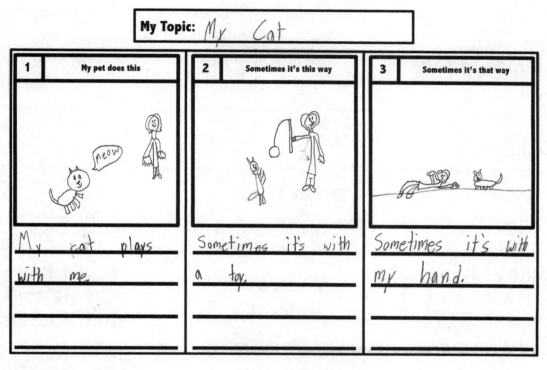

Katelyn Luna, Grade 4

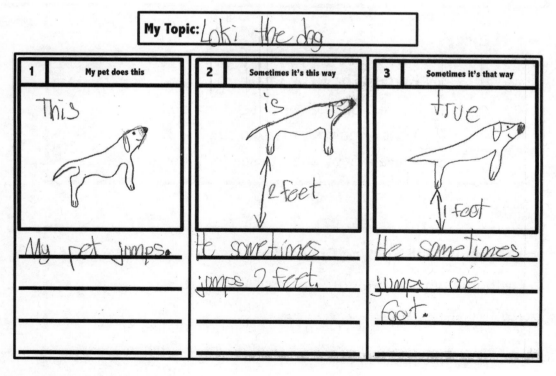

Dailyn Morgan, Grade 4

***Think about something you might decide to sell.***

**Quick List**

- Books or games you don't want anymore
- Food you made
- Toys you want to trade away

**Text Structure**

### For Sale

| What I have for sale and what it costs | Who could use it | What I have for sale and what it costs |

Hot Cross Buns

**Kernel Essay**

**My Kernel: The Baby Chair**

1. I have a baby chair to sell for a dollar.
2. A baby could sit there to eat.
3. I have a baby chair to sell for a dollar.

**Bonus!**

**Grammar and Spelling Connections**

- homophones (*two, to*)
- number words
- exclamation/ announcement
- AAAWWWUBIS (subordinating conjunctions like *after, although, as, while, when, wherever, until, because, if, since*)

## Hot Cross Buns

**H**ot cross buns! Hot cross buns!

One a penny, two a penny, hot cross buns!

**I**f you have no daughters, give them to your sons.

**O**ne a penny, two a penny, hot cross buns!

# STUDENT KERNEL
## For Sale

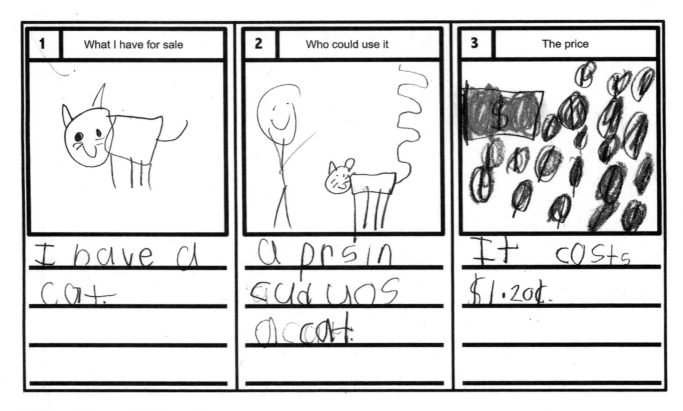

| 1    What I have for sale | 2    Who could use it | 3    The price |
|---|---|---|
| I have a cat. | a prsin suduos a ccat. | It costs $1.20¢. |

William Monge, Kindergarten

# STUDENT KERNEL
## For Sale

| 1  What I have for sale | 2  Who could use it | 3  The price |
|---|---|---|
| I have coke so | Every one loves coca | It costs $400. |

Roselyn Pitner, Kindergarten

| 1  What I have for sale | 2  Who could use it | 3  The price |
|---|---|---|
| I have is crem. | Every one loves is crem. | It costs $3. |

Valeria Santamaria, Kindergarten

# LET'S WRITE!

***Think about times you've hurt yourself or put on a bandage.***

**Quick List**

- Falling off a bike
- Tripping on the stairs
- Hitting your head
- Getting stitches
- Breaking bones

**Text Structure**

### An Accident

| Where I was | What went wrong | How bad it was |

Humpty Dumpty

**Kernel Essay**

**My Kernel: Broken Leg**

1. I was at home, opening presents on Christmas night.
2. I stepped into an empty box and it slid on the floor. I fell and broke my leg.
3. It hurt so much!

**Bonus!**

**Grammar and Spelling Connections**

- **-at, -en** *(sat, men)*
- **y** "e"
- possessives
- contractions
- proper nouns

# Humpty Dumpty

**H**umpty Dumpty sat on a wall,

**H**umpty Dumpty had a great fall.

**A**ll the King's horses and all the King's men

Couldn't put Humpty together again!

# STUDENT KERNEL
## An Accident

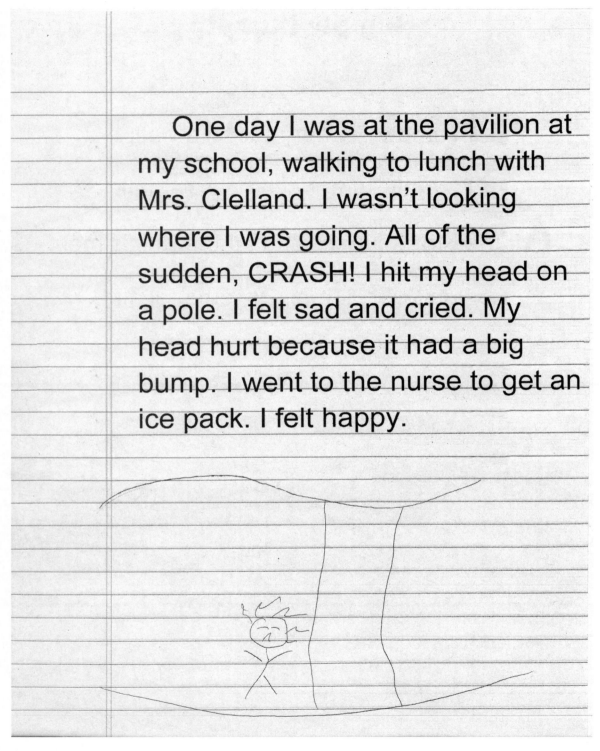

One day I was at the pavilion at my school, walking to lunch with Mrs. Clelland. I wasn't looking where I was going. All of the sudden, CRASH! I hit my head on a pole. I felt sad and cried. My head hurt because it had a big bump. I went to the nurse to get an ice pack. I felt happy.

Paige Eichholtz, Grade 2

# STUDENT KERNEL
## An Accident

**My Topic:** Getting Hurt

| 1   Where I was | 2   What went wrong | 3   How bad it was |
|---|---|---|
| EI was at home. | I skrApt mi nE. | It was so bad! |

Aleia Smith, Kindergarten

**My Topic:** Getting Hurt

| 1   Where I was | 2   What went wrong | 3   How bad it was |
|---|---|---|
| I was at Stre | I sat my lug. | It was so bad! |

Matthew Cubit, Kindergarten

# LET'S WRITE!

*Think about a time when you loaned something and the borrower didn't treat it right. Maybe they gave it back to you broken.*

**Quick List**

- A toy
- A watch
- A book
- A coat
- A pencil

**Text Structure**

### Someone Borrowed My _____

| Someone borrowed my _____ | How they treated it | How I feel about it |
|---|---|---|

I Had a Little Pony

**Kernel Essay**

**My Kernel: My Game**

1. I let my friend take my game home.
2. He scratched the cover.
3. I'm not letting him borrow anything else ever.

**Bonus!**

**Grammar and Spelling Connections**

- double consonant
- possessives
- past tense verbs
- strong verbs
- pitchforking (embedding lists in writing)

## I Had a Little Pony

**I** had a little pony, his name was Dapple-gray,

I lent him to a lady, to ride a mile away.

**S**he whipped him, she slashed him,

She rode him through the mire;

**I** would not lend my pony now

For all the lady's hire.

# STUDENT KERNEL

## Someone Borrowed My _____

**My Topic:** Fidget spinner

| 1  Someone borrowed my — | 2  How they treated it | 3  How I feel about it |
|---|---|---|
| Dylan took my Fidget spinner. | Drew got it back. | Dont let Dylan use it again. |

Billy Clarke, Grade 4

# STUDENT KERNEL
## Someone Borrowed My _____

My Topic: My charm braclet

| 1 Someone borrowed my ____. | 2 How they treated it | 3 How I feel about it |
|---|---|---|
| My sister came in my room and stole my charm braclet. | My charm brack with a charm off it on the fbor. | I feel sad & mad at the same time at Olivia. |

Milly Hernandez, Grade 3

# LET'S WRITE!

*What if you had superpowers? What changes would you make?*

## Quick List

- What if pencils could talk?
- What if flowers could walk?

## Text Structure

### What If

| If . . . | And if . . . | And if . . . | Then . . . ? |
|---|---|---|---|

If All the World Were Apple Pie

## Kernel Essay

**My Kernel: If I Could Go Anywhere**

1. If I could go anywhere . . .
2. And if I could take anybody . . .
3. And if we could stay as long as we wanted . . .
4. Would we ever go to sleep?

## Bonus!

**Grammar and Spelling Connections**

- **ink**
- **ea, ee**
- h brothers (*ch, sh, th*)
- **-id** word family
- *se* vs. *s*
- *cheese* vs. *trees*

- big AAAWWWUBIS (subordinating conjunctions like *after, although, as, while, when, wherever, until, because, if, since*)

# If All the World Were Apple Pie

**I**f all the world were apple pie,

**A**nd all the sea were ink,

**A**nd all the trees were made of cheese,

**W**hat should we have for drink?

# STUDENT KERNEL
## What If

**My Topic:** Pet land

**1 — If...**

i the world were made a toe of puppys.

**2 — And if...**

all the sea had Dogs.

**3 — And if...**

all the flowrs were cats.

**4 — Then...?**

What will be my Pet?

Crystal Berber, Grade 2

# STUDENT KERNEL
## What If

My Topic: The world of food

**1  If...**
the World were bronis.

**2  And if...**
And if all the food were tris.

**3  And if...**
And if all the pipol were gumis.

**4  Then...?**
Then Where I get my fruit?

Katie Kennedy, Grade 2

My Topic: The Word

**1  If...**
the World were puppys.

**2  And if...**
all the sea was Juice

**3  And if...**
all the schools were made of cookes and cream

**4  Then...?**
What should I eat? ice cream!!

Benjamin Berber, Grade 2

# LET'S WRITE!

***Think about pretending to be something.***

### Quick List

- A toy
- An object in the classroom
- An object from your backpack
- An object from the kitchen

### Text Structure

## All About Something—A Description

| What I am and what I look like | My parts | The noise I make | The best thing I do |
|---|---|---|---|

I'm a Little Teapot

### Kernel Essay

**My Kernel: I'm a Birthday Cake**

1. I'm a birthday cake, round and chocolate.
2. I have five candles and icing and cake.
3. I can make people sing "Happy Birthday!"
4. I taste good!

### Bonus!

**Grammar and Spelling Connections**

- homophones (*hear, here*)
- **out**
- **ea**
- I'm
- AAAWWWUBIS (subordinating conjunctions like *after, although, as, while, when, wherever, until, because, if, since*)

## I'm a Little Teapot

I'm a little teapot

Short and stout;

Here is my handle, here is my spout.

When I get all steamed up, hear me shout;

Just tip me over and pour me out!

# STUDENT KERNEL
## All About Something—A Description

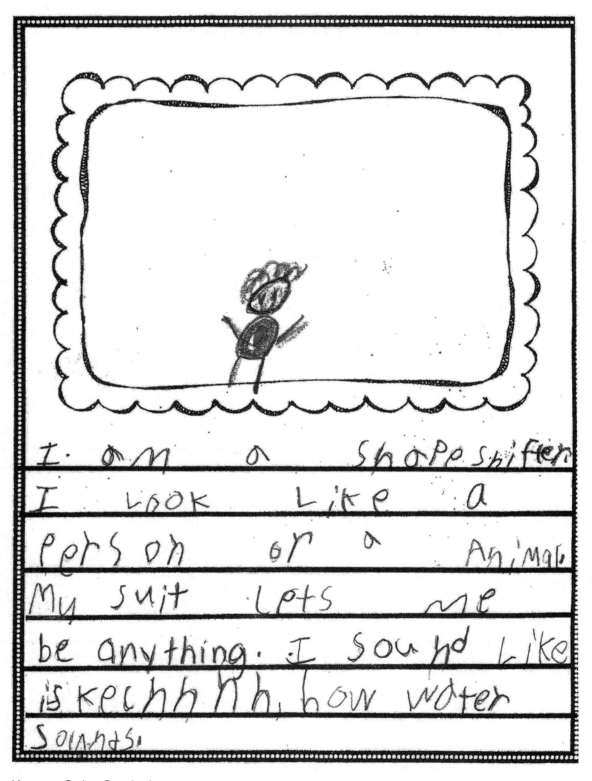

I am a shapeshiften
I look like a
person or a Animal.
My suit lets me
be anything. I sound like
iskechhhhh, how water
sounds.

Karsun Cole, Grade 1

# STUDENT KERNEL
## All About Something—A Description

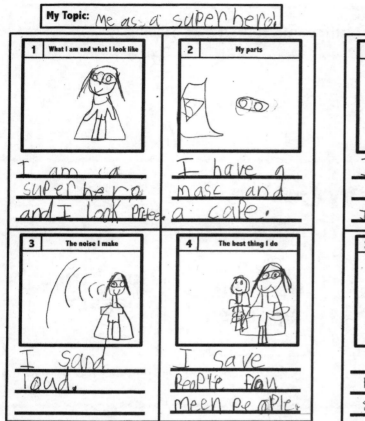

Evelyn Gusman, Grade 1

Savannah Nelson, Grade 1

# LET'S WRITE!

*Think about a time when something got in your way while you were doing something, and it slowed you down.*

**Quick List**

- Getting interrupted
- Having to wait

**Text Structure**

## Try, Try Again

| What I was trying to do | What slowed me down | And then this happened | How I tried again |
|---|---|---|---|

The Itsy Bitsy Spider

**Kernel Essay**

**My Kernel: The Computer**

1. I was playing a game on the computer.
2. The computer screen got stuck.
3. Then I couldn't make anything happen.
4. So my mom rebooted it and I started over.

**Bonus!**

**Grammar and Spelling Connections**

- past tense verbs
- silent letters
- **ai**, **a_e**
- **ow**, **ou**
- y to i
- short and long **i**
- **wa** (*water/washed*)

## The Itsy Bitsy Spider

**T**he itsy bitsy spider climbed up the water spout.

**D**own came the rain and washed the spider out.

**O**ut came the sun and dried up all the rain,

**A**nd the itsy bitsy spider went up the spout again!

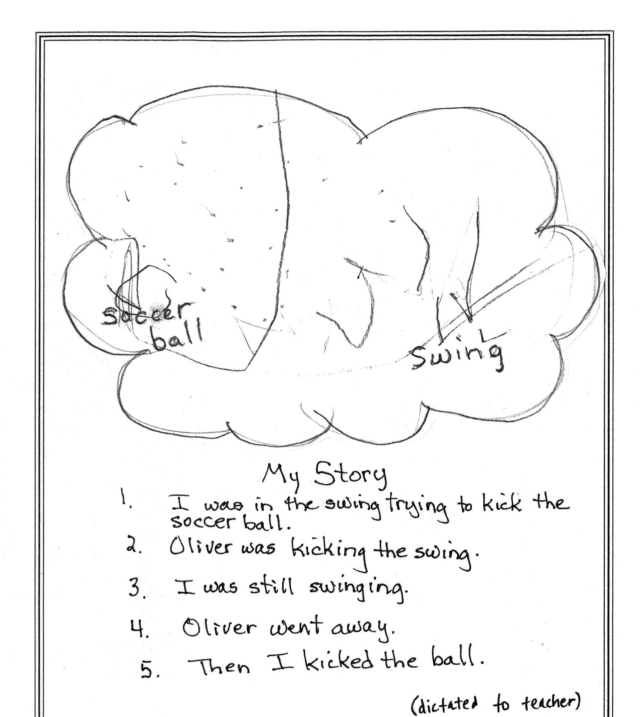

My Story
1. I was in the swing trying to kick the soccer ball.
2. Oliver was kicking the swing.
3. I was still swinging.
4. Oliver went away.
5. Then I kicked the ball.

(dictated to teacher)

Liam Reimer, Prekindergarten

# STUDENT KERNEL

## Try, Try Again

Jimena Ramirez, Grade 2

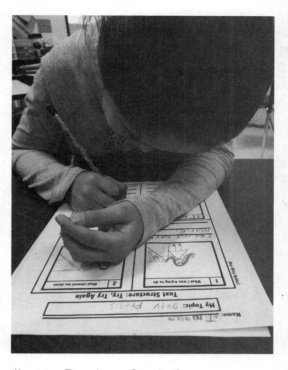

Jimena Ramirez, Grade 2

Isabella Pimentel, Grade 1

Christopher Ramirez, Grade 2

*Think about a time when something bad happened.*

**Quick List**

- You fell on the slide
- A swing hit you in the back
- You dropped your tray in the cafeteria

**Text Structure**

## Ouch! That Hurt!

| What you were doing | But this bad thing happened | And then another bad thing happened |

Jack and Jill

**Kernel Essay**

**My Kernel: Skateboard Accident**

1. I was riding my skateboard while Trink was on a leash.
2. My aunt called me and Trink stopped.
3. The leash tripped me and I skinned my shoulder on the sidewalk.

**Bonus!**

**Grammar and Spelling Connections**

- prepositional phrases
- short vowels
- proper nouns
- **ou**

# Jack and Jill

**J**ack and Jill went up the hill

To fetch a pail of water.

**J**ack fell down and broke his crown,

**A**nd Jill came tumbling after.

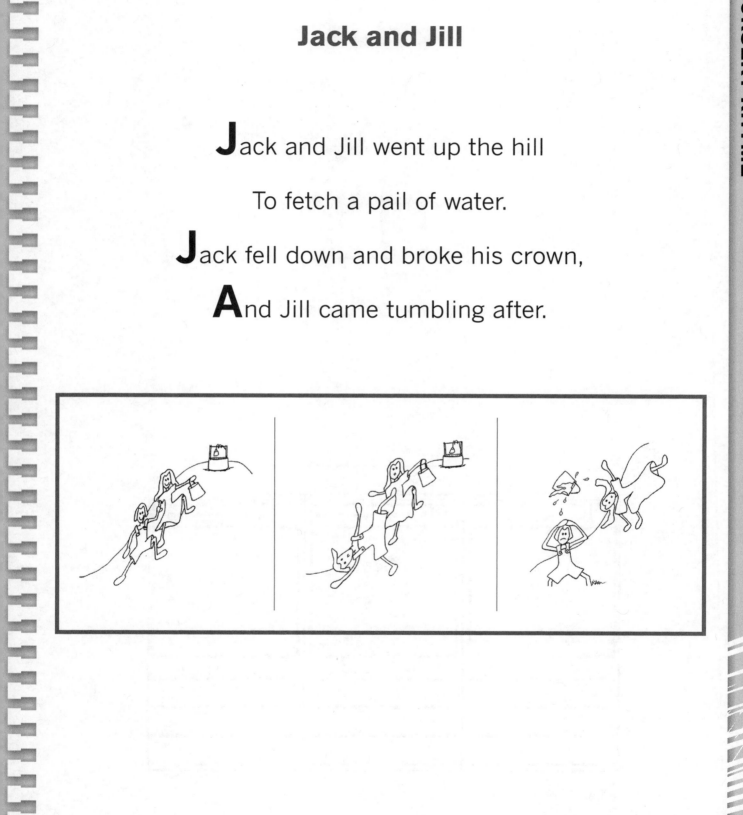

# STUDENT KERNEL
## Ouch! That Hurt!

I was at home when something bit me. I looked and saw it was my toy box.

Austin Lea, Prekindergarten

**My Topic:** Cutting My Toe

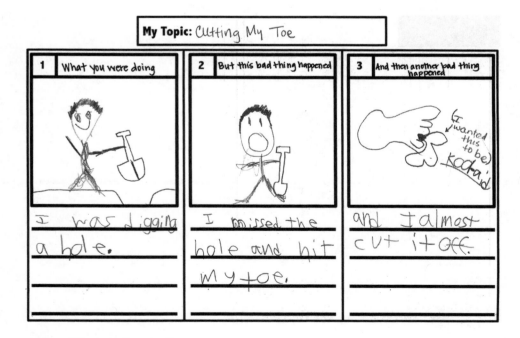

| 1  What you were doing | 2  But this bad thing happened | 3  And then another bad thing happened |
|---|---|---|
| I was digging a hole. | I missed the hole and hit my toe. | and I almost cut it off. (I wanted this to be) kodaid |

Julian Ponce, Grade 5

# STUDENT KERNEL
## Ouch! That Hurt!

My Topic: Chato biting me.

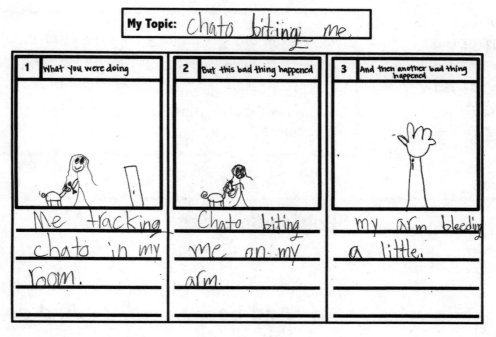

| 1 What you were doing | 2 But this bad thing happened | 3 And then another bad thing happened |
|---|---|---|
| Me tracking chato in my room. | Chato biting me on my arm. | my arm bleeding a little. |

Lily Keyes, Grade 3

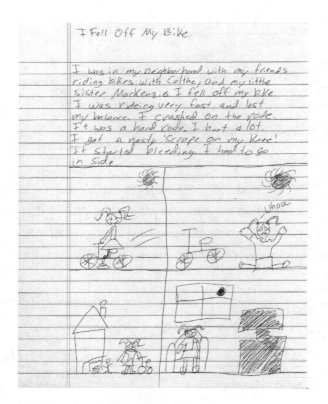

I Fell Off My Bike.

I was in my neighborhood with my friends riding bikes with Colthe, and my little sister Mackenzia. I fell off my bike. I was rideing very fast and lost my balance. I crashed on the rode. It was a hard rode. I hurt a lot. I got a nasty scrape on my knee! It started bleeding. I had to go in side.

Natalie Cortez, Grade 2

# LET'S WRITE!

*Think about a time when you gave someone advice about how to be good at something.*

## Quick List

- How to answer politely
- How to raise your hand
- How to walk down the hall without getting in trouble
- How to kick a soccer ball
- How to be a leader

## Text Structure

**Helping Someone**

| Be this . . . | And be this . . . | And do this . . . |
|---|---|---|

Jack Be Nimble

## Kernel Essay

**My Kernel: Helping With Groceries**

1. Be helpful . . .
2. And be fast . . .
3. And get the rest of the bags out of the car while your mom is putting away the groceries.

## Bonus!

**Grammar and Spelling Connections**

- **ck**
- adjectives
- compound words
- direct address
- commands
- **le**

## Jack Be Nimble

**J**ack be nimble,

**J**ack be quick;

**J**ack jump over

The candlestick.

# STUDENT KERNEL
## Helping Someone

**My Topic:** hlPing my SiSr

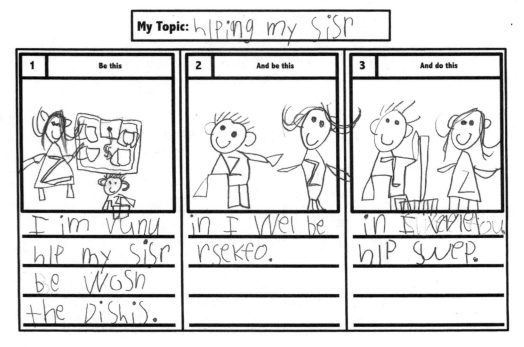

| 1 Be this | 2 And be this | 3 And do this |
|---|---|---|
| I im vuny hlP my SiSr be WaSh the DiShiS. | in I Wel be rsekfo. | in Fixavleou hlP swep. |

Joseph Edwards, Grade 1

**My Topic:** PoP ChidhiP

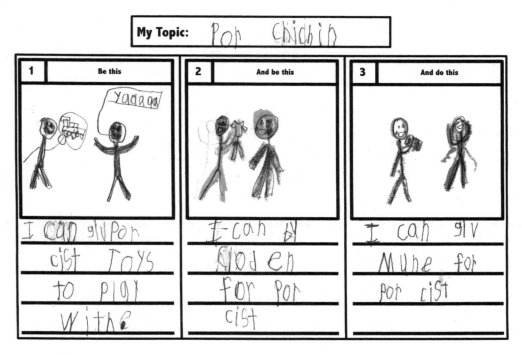

| 1 Be this | 2 And be this | 3 And do this |
|---|---|---|
| I can glvPor cist Toys to Plal Withe | I can by Nod en for Por cist | I can giv Mune for Por cist |

Chase Cipriano, Grade 1

# STUDENT KERNEL
## Helping Someone

**My Topic:** CUSINS

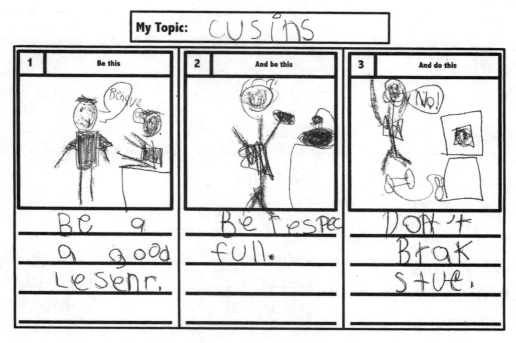

Gabriel Dominguez, Grade 1

**My Topic:** in the school

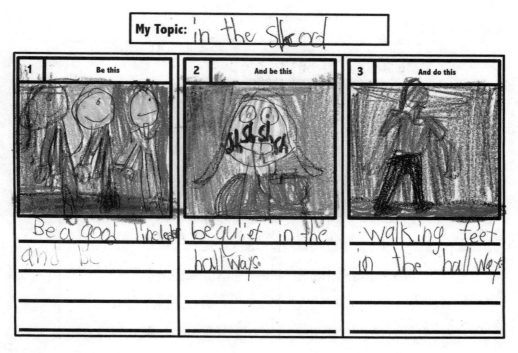

Emily Cherry, Grade 1

**Think about how you and someone else like different parts of something.**

### Quick List

- Pizza/crust
- Cake/icing
- Round/square Lego pieces

### Text Structure

**Win–Win**

| One person's problem | Another person's problem | One thing that solved both problems |

Jack Sprat

### Kernel Essay

**My Kernel: Oreos**

1. My mom doesn't like the white part.
2. I don't like the cookie part.
3. So we split the cookie and she eats the outside and I eat the inside.

### Bonus!

**Grammar and Spelling Connections**

- **ea**
- pronouns (*them, they, his*)
- opposites
- short **a**
- long **o**

# Jack Sprat

**J**ack Sprat could eat no fat,

**H**is wife could eat no lean;

And so, between them both,

**T**hey licked the platter clean.

Me and lizzie both want the swing so we take turns pushing and riding.

Abigail James, Grade 3

# STUDENT KERNEL
## Win-Win

Me and my mom take turns in the Kayak and riding around in the tube pulled by the Kayak.

Elizabeth Hicks, Grade 5

# LET'S WRITE!

*Think about an emergency that happened somewhere.*

**Quick List**

- A hurricane
- A flood
- A fire

**Text Structure**

## News Report

| This emergency just happened | What it caused | Some good news |
|---|---|---|

Ladybug, Ladybug

**Kernel Essay**

**My Kernel: Hailstorm!**

1. We just had hail outside!
2. It made dents in the cars.
3. The cars still work, though!

**Bonus!**

**Grammar and Spelling Connections**

- synonyms (*house, home; gone, crept*)
- proper nouns
- compound words

## Ladybug, Ladybug

**L**adybug, Ladybug, fly away home,

**Y**our house is on fire, your children all gone,

**A**ll but one, and her name is Ann,

And she crept under the pudding-pan.

# STUDENT KERNEL
## News Report

Chase Cipriano, Grade 1

# STUDENT KERNEL
## News Report

**My Topic:** Dythr omost Drowe.

| 1 This emergency just happened | 2 What it caused | 3 Some good news |
|---|---|---|
| my Duthr omost Drown | my Granalmom was wored | but wtih's boy I Saved my Duthr. |

Nesarae Wolf, Grade 1

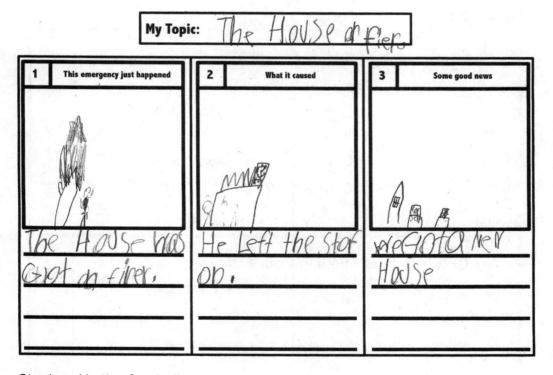

**My Topic:** The House on fier.

| 1 This emergency just happened | 2 What it caused | 3 Some good news |
|---|---|---|
| The House nes Guot an fier. | He Left the staf on. | weGtota ner House |

Stephen Urrtia, Grade 1

# LET'S WRITE!

**Think about something that you lost.**

## Quick List

- Your cat
- Your game charger
- Your lunch money

## Text Structure

### Something Is Lost—Problem/Solution

| I lost _____. | That means I can't _____. | So I think I will do this . . . | . . . and this will happen. |

Little Bo Peep

## Kernel Essay

**My Kernel: My Blanket**

1. I lost my blanket.
2. That means I can't go to sleep.
3. I will look for it.
4. And I will find it somewhere.

## Bonus!

**Grammar and Spelling Connections**

- **eep**
- short **a**
- long **o**
- double consonant + -ing
- contractions
- past vs. future tense
- **ee** vs. **ea**
- pronouns

**NURSERY RHYME**

## Little Bo Peep

**L**ittle Bo Peep has lost her sheep,

**A**nd doesn't know where to find them.

**L**eave them alone and they'll come home,

**W**agging their tails behind them.

## Something Is Lost—Problem/Solution

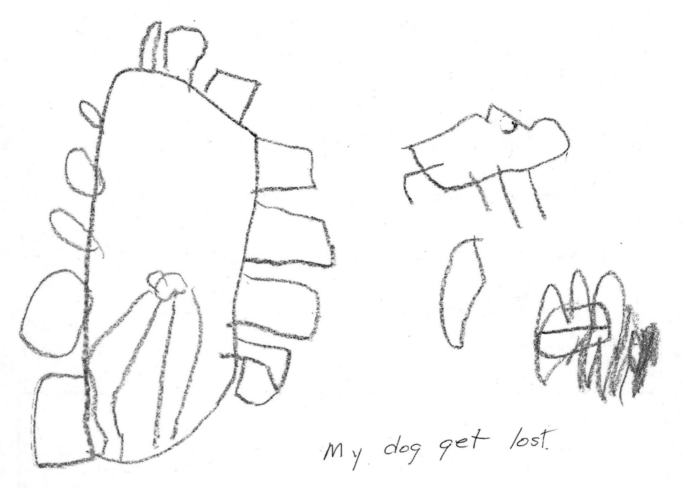

My dog get lost.

Josiah Opina, Prekindergarten

# STUDENT KERNEL
## Something Is Lost—Problem/Solution

My Topic: race

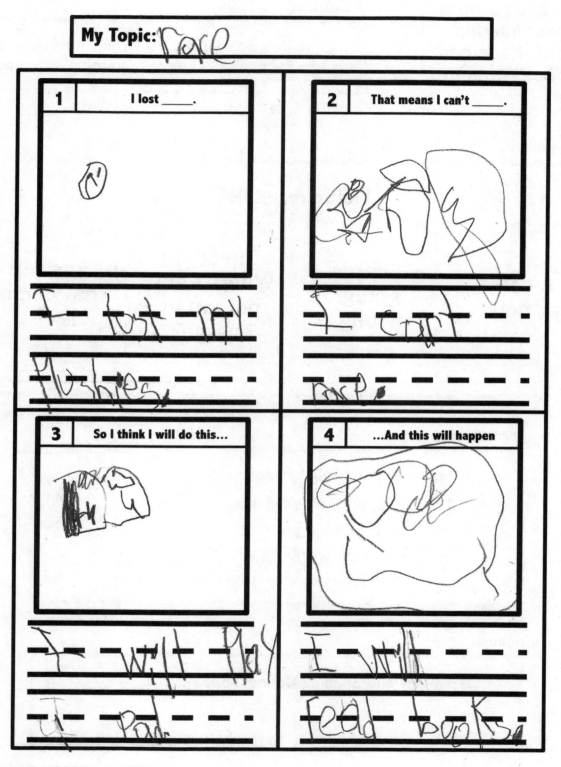

**1** | I lost ____.

I lost my Flushies.

**2** | That means I can't ____.

I can't race.

**3** | So I think I will do this...

I will Play I Pad.

**4** | ...And this will happen

I will read books.

Rory Shook, Kindergarten

# LET'S WRITE!

*Think about a time when you needed help, but it seemed like nobody was in charge.*

**Quick List**

- There's no cashier at the store
- There's no teacher on the playground

**Text Structure**

## What a Mess! Help!

| A call for help | What is going wrong | Question: Where's the person in charge? | Answer: That person is . . . |

Little Boy Blue

**Kernel Essay**

**My Kernel: No Toilet Paper!**

1. Help! I need some toilet paper!
2. I'm in the bathroom.
3. Mom, where are you?
4. She's in the back yard, watering the garden.

**Bonus!**

**Grammar and Spelling Connections**

- contractions
- **ou**
- **or**
- digraphs
- preposition

## Little Boy Blue

**L**ittle Boy Blue come blow your horn,

**T**he sheep's in the meadow, the cow's in the corn.

**B**ut where's the boy who looks after the sheep?

**H**e's under a haystack fast asleep.

# STUDENT KERNEL

## What a Mess! Help!

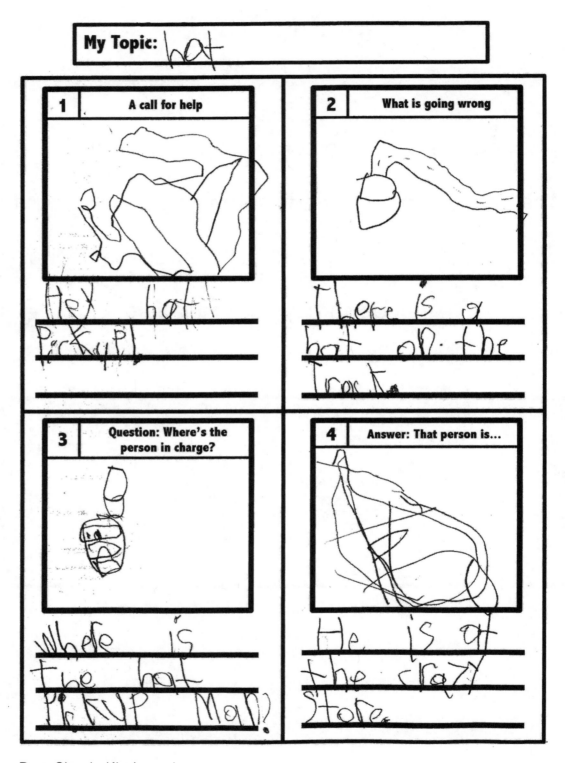

**My Topic:** hat

**1  A call for help**

Hex hot
PickuPl

**2  What is going wrong**

There is a
hot on the
Tract

**3  Question: Where's the person in charge?**

Where is
the hot
PickuP Man?

**4  Answer: That person is...**

He is ot
the crazy
Store.

Rory Shook, Kindergarten

# STUDENT KERNEL
## What a Mess! Help!

Me and Tatum made a mess, playing. We had toys everywhere and stuffed animals. No one helped me. I cleaned it. And I said, "Finally!"

Olivia Keyes, Prekindergarten

# LET'S WRITE!

***Think about a time you did a good job.***

**Quick List**

- You did some nice work
- You cleaned your room
- You built something great

**Text Structure**

## Good Job!

| Where I was | What I was doing | What I did | Something nice someone said |

Little Jack Horner

**Kernel Essay**

**My Kernel: Reading a Book**

1. I was sitting on my bed.
2. I was looking at a book.
3. I read some of the words.
4. My grandma said she didn't know I could do that!

**Bonus!**

**Grammar and Spelling Connections**

- capitalize holidays
- double **l**
- silent **b**
- quotation marks
- capitalize **l**
- participial phrases

## Little Jack Horner

**L**ittle Jack Horner sat in the corner

**E**ating his Christmas pie.

**H**e put in his thumb and pulled out a plum

**A**nd said, "What a good boy am I!"

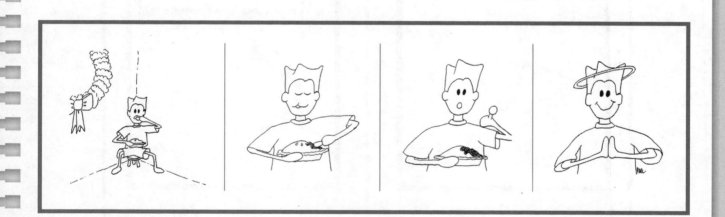

# STUDENT KERNEL
## Good Job!

| 1 | Where I was |
|---|---|

I was at school.

| 2 | What I was doing |
|---|---|

I was im CEIE

| 3 | What I did |
|---|---|

I was CET super star.

| 4 | Something nice someone said |
|---|---|

Ms. Gibson said good job and

Kasey Malagarie, Kindergarten

# STUDENT KERNEL
## Good Job!

**1** Where I was

I was at school.

**2** What I was doing

I rus on pink.

**3** What I did

I was being good.

**4** Something nice someone said

Good job.

Matthew Cubit, Kindergarten

# LET'S WRITE!

**Think about a feeling you have had.**

**Quick List**

- Happy
- Sad
- Mad
- Confused

**Text Structure**

## Defining a Feeling

My name is . . .

When I feel . . .

That means . . .

Little Jumping Joan

**Kernel Essay**

**My Kernel: Matilde**

1. My name is Matilde.
2. When I feel sad . . .
3. . . . that means I need to sing something.

**Bonus!**

**Grammar and Spelling Connections**

- alliteration
- contractions
- word order
  (Here am I)
- AAAWWWUBIS
  (subordinating
  conjunctions like *after,
  although, as, while,
  when, wherever, until,
  because, if, since*)

## Little Jumping Joan

**H**ere am I, little jumping Joan;
**W**hen nobody's with me,
**I**'m always alone.

## Defining a Feeling

Lily Keyes, Grade 3

I Am olivia. When I get mad I tell my friend Tatum to not come by me.

Olivia Keyes, Prekindergarten

***Think about a time
when you experienced
a problem.***

**Quick List**

- You couldn't find your materials
- Something went wrong at home
- You got into an argument with your friend

**Text Structure**

## My Short Story

| | | |
|---|---|---|
| **What you were doing** | **But suddenly a problem came up** | **What you did about it** |

Little Miss Muffet

**Kernel Essay**

**My Kernel: The Jetties**

1. I was climbing the rocks at the jetties.
2. A big wave splashed up through the rocks.
3. I stepped back and went another way.

**Bonus!**

**Grammar and Spelling Connections**

- **-at** family
- irregular verbs
- proper nouns
- double consonants

## Little Miss Muffet

**L**ittle Miss Muffet sat on a tuffet

Eating her curds and whey;

**A**long came a spider

Who sat down beside her

**A**nd frightened Miss Muffet away.

# STUDENT KERNEL
## My Short Story

I was at home playing with
my friend, and we knocked over
the lamp that was in my room
and it broke. I was very scared.
I ran to my mommy who then
cleaned it up with the vaccum.

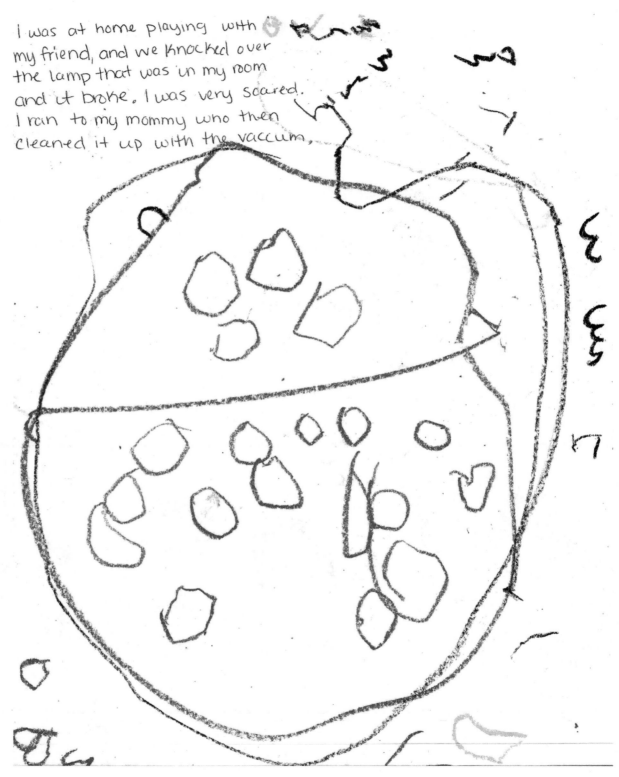

Brayden Anderson, Prekindergarten

# STUDENT KERNEL
## My Short Story

### Little mister Zachary

Little mister zachary was Playing
tag then I was chasing my friend along came
a sqorpin then it fallon'd me then I ran away.

Zachary Meyn, Grade 1

### Little miss Natalie

Little miss. Natalie was playing out
Side casing her friends around, along came a
Cat and scerd on to a swing It got clouser
and clouser. and I was not seerd any more.

Natalie Cortez, Grade 1

# LET'S WRITE!

*Think about a time someone did something, and you wanted to know more about it.*

## Quick List

- Your friend drew something
- Your cousin went somewhere
- Your friend walked away from you on the playground
- Someone got hurt

## Text Structure

### Three Questions

| Someone did something | One thing I want to know about it | Another thing I want to know about it | And one more thing I want to know |

Little Tommy Tucker

## Kernel Essay

**My Kernel: The Amish Lady**

1. The Amish lady sold us a pumpkin.
2. Did she grow all of these pumpkins?
3. Does she always wear a bonnet?
4. Does she ever drive a car, or just the horse buggy?

## Bonus!

**Grammar and Spelling Connections**

- double consonants
- questions
- alliteration
- compound words

## Little Tommy Tucker

**L**ittle Tommy Tucker sings for his supper.

**W**hat shall he eat? White bread and butter.

**H**ow shall he cut it without any knife?

**H**ow shall he marry without any wife?

# STUDENT KERNEL
## Three Questions

**My Topic:** LiTTLe Jorann.

**1 Someone did something**

Jordan plays guitar for friends

**2 One thing I want to know about it**

Shall he play rock or country?

**3 Another thing I want to know about it**

How shall he play fast or slow?

**4 And one more thing I want to know**

How will he play without a band

Jordan Redman, Grade 1

# STUDENT KERNEL
## Three Questions

My Topic: MomCooks

**1** | Someone did something

Mom is cooking for her children.

**2** | One thing I want to know about it

Shall she cook bacon or chicken?

**3** | Another thing I want to know about it

How shall she cook without a stove?

**4** | And one more thing I want to know

Will she become a chep?

Latrell Lafond, Grade 1

# LET'S WRITE!

***Think about a time you lost something and then found it.***

### Quick List

- A toy
- Game tokens
- Pencil
- A lost tooth
- A coat

### Text Structure

## I Lost Something!

| I lost my _____. | Someone who helped me look for it | What we found | What I got back |

Lucy Locket

### Kernel Essay

**My Kernel: My Lost Camera**

1. I lost my camera.
2. My mom helped me look for it.
3. We found the case.
4. And then I found the camera.

### Bonus!

**Grammar and Spelling Connections**

- double consonants
- alliteration
- ck
- pronoun "it"

## Lucy Locket

**L**ucy Locket lost her pocket,

**K**itty Fisher found it;

**N**ot a penny was there in it,

**O**nly ribbon round it.

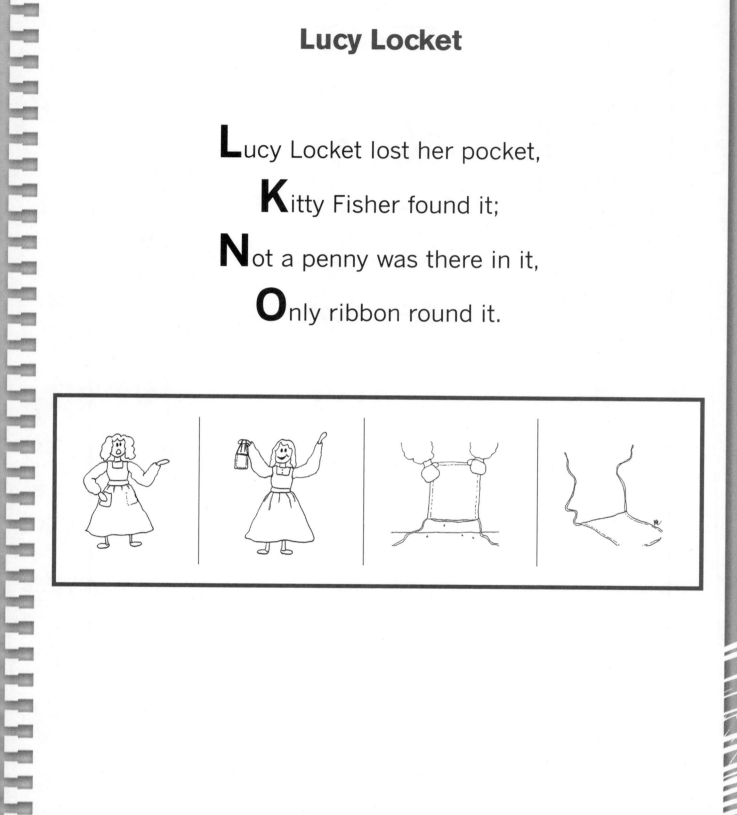

# STUDENT KERNEL
## I Lost Something!

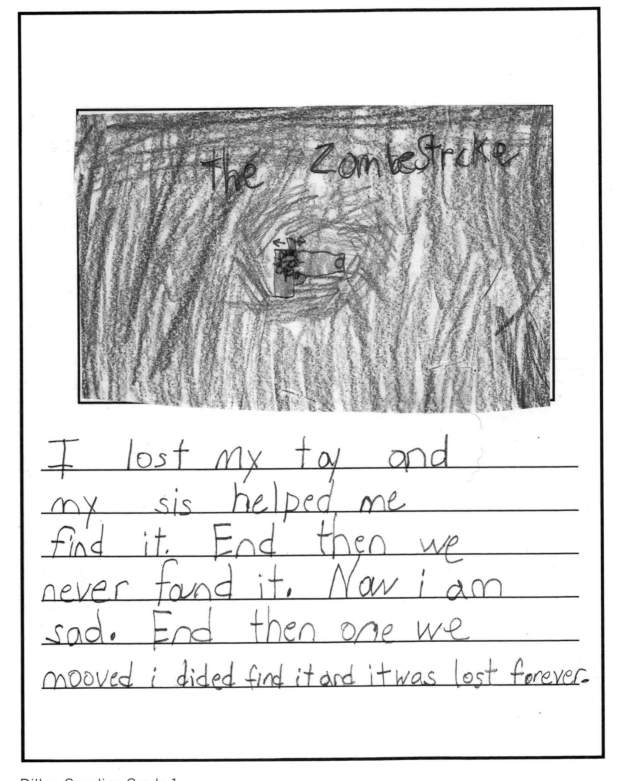

The ZombeStrcke

I lost my toy and
my sis helped me
find it. End then we
never fand it. Naw i am
sad. End then one we
mooved i dided find it and it was lost forever.

Dillon Cuvelier, Grade 1

# STUDENT KERNEL
## I Lost Something!

Londyn Johnson lost her ring, Megan Trainor found it, not a dimonad was on it, only trash was around it.

Londyn Johnson, Grade 3

**Think about some of your favorite possessions.**

### Quick List

- A toy
- A game
- A color
- A pencil
- A pet

### Text Structure

## Prized Possession

| What I have | What it looks like | The best thing about it | One time . . . |

Mary Had a Little Lamb

### Kernel Essay

**My Kernel: My Dog Foxy**

1. I have a dog named Foxy.
2. She is reddish with a long tail.
3. She loves me and sleeps near me.
4. One time she ran away because she was scared of the fireworks outside but she came home after 13 days.

### Bonus!

**Grammar and Spelling Connections**

- silent **b, gh**
- similes
- its
- **wh**
- long vowels
- different **ch** sounds (*school, children*)

## Mary Had a Little Lamb

**M**ary had a little lamb, **i**ts fleece
was white as snow;

**A**nd everywhere that Mary went,
the lamb was sure to go.

**I**t followed her to school one day,
which was against the rule;

It made the children laugh and play
to see a lamb at school.

# STUDENT KERNEL
## Prized Possession

One time Lola had a drown dog. she wod pefit

Sayleigh Sotomayor, Kindergarten

My Topic: The Pupe

1 What I have

I have a Pupe.

2 What it looks like

Pupe has ear.

3 The best thing about it

is plas with me.

4 One time...

I barung my pupe in my room.

Ryan Nieto, Grade 2

# STUDENT KERNEL
## Prized Possession

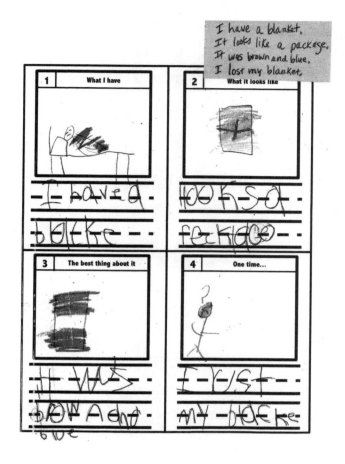

I have a blanket.
It looks like a package.
It was brown and blue.
I lost my blanket.

Jovan Ramirez, Grade 1

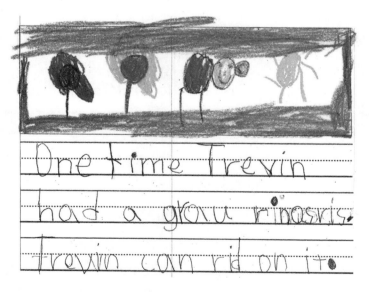

Hank Barnes, Kindergarten

# LET'S WRITE!

*Think of someone you'd like to politely talk to, maybe someone you'd like to get to know better.*

**Quick List**

- Classmate
- Relative
- Adult

**Text Structure**

## Polite Q and A

| Name of person you're talking to | Question: How is your . . . doing? | Answers: 1. 2. 3. |

Mary, Mary, Quite Contrary

**Kernel Essay**

**My Kernel: My Opa**

1. Opa, Opa . . .
2. How is your sailboat doing?
3. The sails are fine, the ropes are all coiled, and the cabin is ready for visitors!

**Bonus!**

**Grammar and Spelling Connections**

- alliteration
- adjectives
- **ow**
- blends
- **ell**
- direct address
- pitchforking (embedding lists in writing)

# Mary, Mary, Quite Contrary

**M**ary, Mary, quite contrary,

**H**ow does your garden grow?

**W**ith silver bells and cockle shells,

And pretty maids all in a row.

"Hey mother lilly,"
"How is your dog?"
"He is growing, eating, and playing."

Bella Martinez, Grade 4

# STUDENT KERNEL
## Polite Q and A

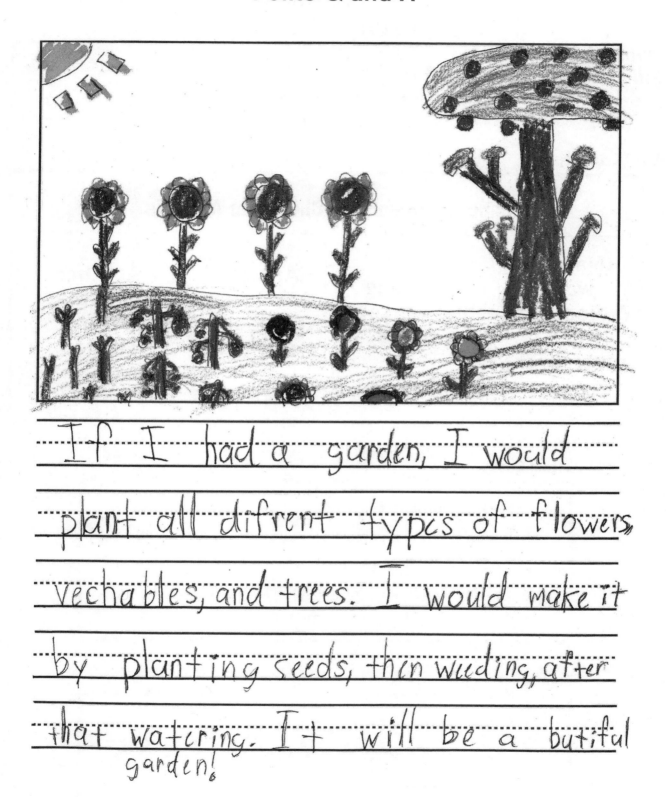

If I had a garden, I would plant all difrent types of flowers, vechables, and trees. I would make it by planting seeds, then wuding, after that watcring. It will be a butiful garden!

Jacob Murray, Grade 1

# LET'S WRITE!

### Quick List

*Think of someone you know well.*

*Arroz con leche*

- Friend
- Family member
- Neighbor
- Relative

### Text Structure

**All About Someone—A Character Analysis**

| (Name) was (adjective) [then reverse it] | One thing that person wanted | Another thing that person wanted | Another thing that person wanted |

Old King Cole

### Kernel Essay

**My Kernel: Aunt Sue**

1. Aunt Sue is a gardener; a gardener is Aunt Sue.
2. She wants her garden gloves.
3. She likes to use her garden digger.
4. And then she wants some unsweet tea.

### Bonus!

**Grammar and Spelling Connections**

- order of words
- double consonants
- adjectives
- **ou**, **ow**

## Old King Cole

**O**ld King Cole was a merry old soul,

And a merry old soul was he;

**H**e called for his pipe,

**A**nd he called for his bowl,

**A**nd he called for his fiddlers three.

# STUDENT KERNEL
## All About Someone—A Character Analysis

**My Topic:** Mr. Twinkles And Butterscotch

| | |
|---|---|
| **1** (Name) was (adjective) (then reverse it) | **2** One thing that person wanted |
| | hayintheball |
| Mr. Twinkles and Butterscotch are babys. Babys are Butterscotch and Mr Twinkles. | Mr. Twinkles and Butter Scotch want food. |
| **3** Another thing that person wanted | **4** Another thing that person wanted |
| | |
| Mr. Twinkles and Butterscotch wanted water. | Mr. Twinkles and Butter Scotch wanted love. |

Ava Lacey, Grade 2

# STUDENT KERNEL
## All About Someone—A Character Analysis

**My Topic:** My cuson Tristen

**1** (Name) was (adjective) (then reverse it)

Tristen is funny. Funny is tristen.

**2** One thing that person wanted

HA HA HA

Tristen wants to make people laufe.

**3** Another thing that person wanted

Bird Drone

Tristen wants a drone.

**4** Another thing that person wanted

tristen wants iccreamafter his baseball games.

Peyton Vann, Grade 2

# LET'S WRITE!

***Think of a time you were disappointed—when something didn't go your way.***

## Quick List

- You get told "no" at the store
- Something you are trying to buy is sold out
- Someone doesn't get to come over after all
- Your food isn't as good as you wanted it to be

## Text Structure

### A Disappointment

| Where you went | What you wanted there | What you found there | What you think about that |
|---|---|---|---|

Old Mother Hubbard

## Kernel Essay

**My Kernel: Spice Girls Concert**

1. We went online.
2. We wanted to buy tickets to a Spice Girls concert.
3. But they were sold out already.
4. So we never thought we'd ever get to see the Spice Girls.

## Bonus!

**Grammar and Spelling Connections**

- double consonants
- **-one** (*bone, none*)
- long vowels
- pronouns

- AAAWWWUBIS (subordinating conjunctions like *after, although, as, while, when, wherever, until, because, if, since*)

## Old Mother Hubbard

**O**ld Mother Hubbard went to the cupboard

**T**o get her poor doggy a bone.

**W**hen she got there, the cupboard was bare,

**S**o the poor doggy had none.

# STUDENT KERNEL

## A Disappointment

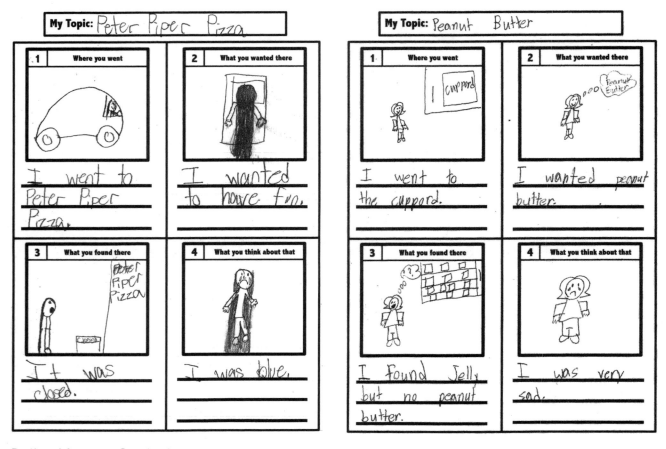

**My Topic:** Peter Piper Pizza

| 1 — Where you went | 2 — What you wanted there |
|---|---|
| I went to Peter Piper Pizza. | I wanted to have fun. |

| 3 — What you found there | 4 — What you think about that |
|---|---|
| It was closed. | I was blue. |

Dailyn Morgan, Grade 4

**My Topic:** Peanut Butter

| 1 — Where you went | 2 — What you wanted there |
|---|---|
| I went to the cuppard. | I wanted peanut butter. |

| 3 — What you found there | 4 — What you think about that |
|---|---|
| I found Jelly but no peanut butter. | I was very sad. |

Katelyn Luna, Grade 4

# STUDENT KERNEL
## A Disappointment

We took a trip to see the dogwoods blooming. We wanted to see the woods looking like a fairyland. When we got there, we saw no white flowers at all, but just green forest instead. We realized with disappointment that the warm winter made them bloom earlier.

Dixie Shoopman, Author's Mother

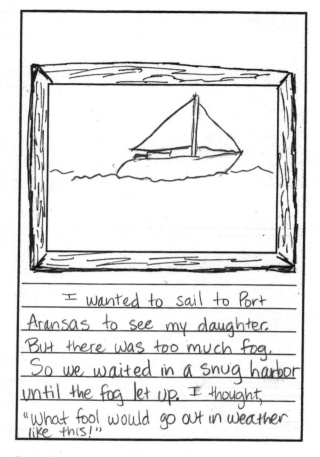

I wanted to sail to Port Aransas to see my daughter. But there was too much fog. So we waited in a snug harbor until the fog let up. I thought, "What fool would go out in weather like this!"

Bert Shoopman, Author's Father

# LET'S WRITE!

***Think of a time you made something.***

## Quick List

- Arts and crafts
- Cookies
- A gift

## Text Structure

### Making Something

| What we will make | Step 1 | Step 2 | Step 3 |

Pat-a-Cake,
Pat-a-Cake

## Kernel Essay

**My Kernel: A Slingshot**

1. We will make a small and powerful slingshot.
2. First we cut the top off a plastic bottle and keep it.
3. Next we cut the top off a balloon and keep the bottom.
4. Then we use a rubber band to fasten the balloon to the bottletop. Now we can shoot things!

## Bonus!

**Grammar and Spelling Connections**

- **ake**
- pronouns
- *cvc* (consonant-vowel-consonant) words
- **an**
- blends
- long vowels

## Pat-a-Cake, Pat-a-Cake

**P**at-a-cake, pat-a-cake, baker's man,

Bake me a cake as fast as you can;

**P**at it and prick it and **m**ark it with a "B,"

**A**nd put it in the oven for baby and me.

# STUDENT KERNEL
## Making Something

My Topic: Mizanin's Magic Perfume (MMP)

**1 What we will make**

We will make my scent changing perfume.

**2 Step 1**

First get a pretty bottle and cap (depends on how much you want.)

**3 Step 2**

Then, get 1 c. of water and whatever you want your perfume to smell like.

**4 Step 3**

Mix them together in the bottle and buy my magic buttons and lable ($1 each)

This is the most awsome perfume ever! If you want idea's go to Miz.com/cute!

Erica Mizanin, Grade 3

# STUDENT KERNEL
## Making Something

My Topic: How to make a Pizza

| 1 | What we will make |
|---|---|

We will make a pizza.

| 2 | Step 1 |
|---|---|

We will get some pizza dogh

| 3 | Step 2 |
|---|---|

We will put pizza sauce and cheese on pizza doah.

| 4 | Step 3 |
|---|---|

We will put pizza on a pan and bake.

Pizza is my favorite food!

Jack Watson, Grade 3

# LET'S WRITE!

*Think of something you like in many different ways.*

## Quick List

- Lego designs
- Ice cream toppings
- Chips and dips
- Games you play outside

## Text Structure

### Three Ways It Can Be

| The first way | The second way | The third way |
|---|---|---|

Pease Porridge Hot

## Kernel Essay

**My Kernel: Swings**

1. Swings can be wooden and on long ropes hanging from a tall tree.
2. Or they can be flat, wide, and twisty.
3. Or they can be shaped like a disk with one rope through the middle.

## Bonus!

**Grammar and Spelling Connections**

- alliteration
- short **e**
- irregular verbs (keep/kept)
- word order
- **-ot** word family

## Pease Porridge Hot

**P**ease porridge hot, **p**ease porridge cold,
**P**ease porridge in the pot—nine days old.

Some like it hot, some like it cold,

Some like it in the pot—nine days old.

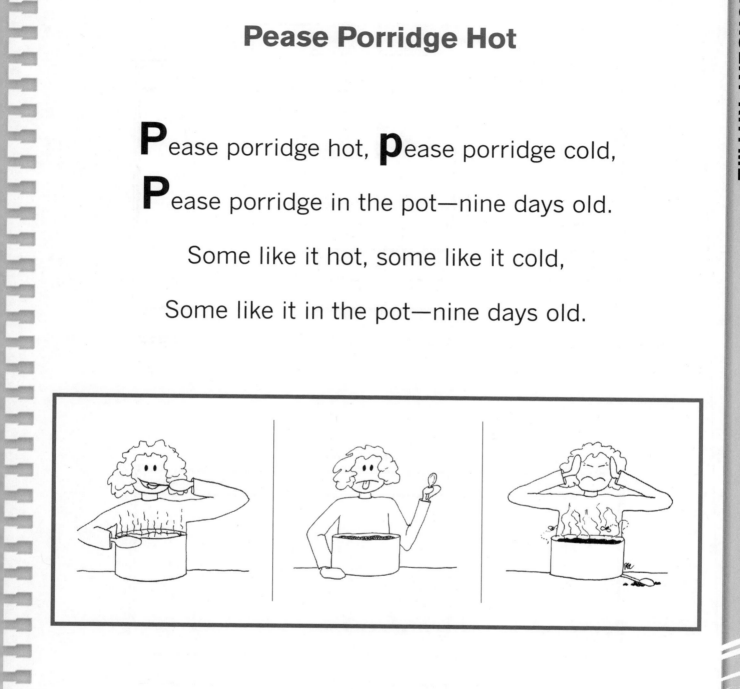

# STUDENT KERNEL

## Three Ways It Can Be

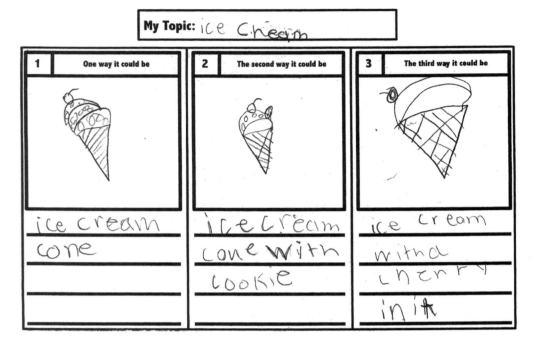

**My Topic:** ice cream

| 1 One way it could be | 2 The second way it could be | 3 The third way it could be |
|---|---|---|
| ice cream cone | ice cream cone with cookie | ice cream with a cherry in it |

Samantha Inmon, Grade 2

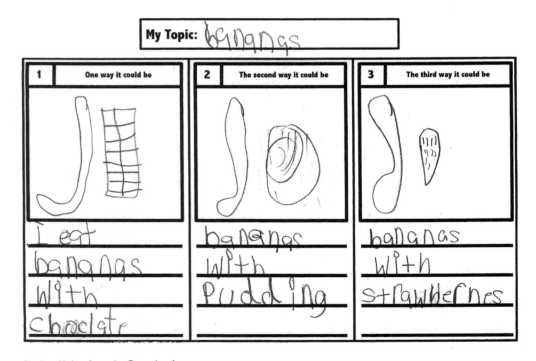

**My Topic:** bananas

| 1 One way it could be | 2 The second way it could be | 3 The third way it could be |
|---|---|---|
| I eat bananas with choclate | bananas with pudding | bananas with strawberries |

Latrell Lafond, Grade 1

# STUDENT KERNEL
## Three Ways It Can Be

My Topic: Chips

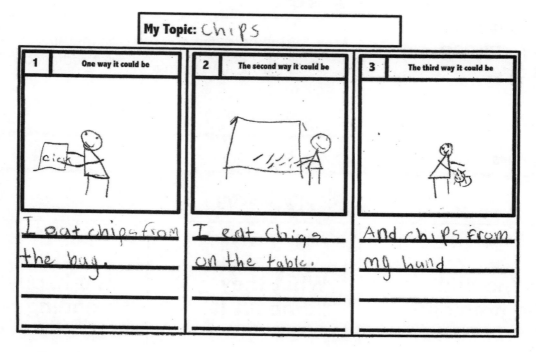

| 1 One way it could be | 2 The second way it could be | 3 The third way it could be |
|---|---|---|
| I eat chips from the bag. | I eat chips on the table. | And chips from my hand |

Amaya Garcia, Grade 1

My Topic: cholate

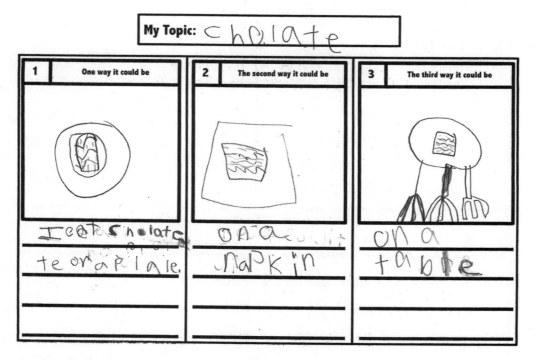

| 1 One way it could be | 2 The second way it could be | 3 The third way it could be |
|---|---|---|
| I eat cholate te or a plate. | on a napkin | on a table |

Jordan Redman, Grade 1

# LET'S WRITE!

*Think about a time a problem turned out just fine.*

**Quick List**

- Winning a game
- Building something
- Weather changing for the better
- Something broken got replaced

**Text Structure**

## Happy Ending

| Who had the problem | What they did about it | The happy ending |

Peter, Peter, Pumpkin Eater

**Kernel Essay**

**My Kernel: The School Project**

1. Julian didn't want to start his project.
2. He waited until it was due.
3. When he finally got started, it was actually interesting and fun and easy.

**Bonus!**

**Grammar and Spelling Connections**

- alliteration
- double consonant
- past tense
- **-er**

## Peter, Peter, Pumpkin Eater

**P**eter, Peter, pumpkin eater,

Had a wife and couldn't keep her!

**H**e put her in a pumpkin shell,

**A**nd there he kept her very well!

# STUDENT KERNEL
## Happy Ending

### The Easter Bunny's Assistant

| | |
|---|---|
| Who had the problem? | The bunny was trying to explain how to dye eggs but the skunk kept getting excited. |
| What they did about it: | The bunny pushed him outside so it would not stink. |
| The happy ending: | The bunny felt bad, so he put a clothespin on his nose and let skunk back in. |

Shannon String, Kindergarten

### Jamie O'Rourke

| | | |
|---|---|---|
| Who had the problem: | Jamie took a seed from a leprechaun. | Jamie's wife was hurt and couldn't work. |
| What they did about it: | His plant grew the biggest potato ever, and it got stuck in the village. | The villagers dug and cut up the large potatoes |
| The happy ending: | He never had to worry about planting again. | He got the villagers to do all of the work. |

Shannon String, Kindergarten

# STUDENT KERNEL
## Happy Ending

Everyone is running away from the bad guys.
The powerrangers saved the day.

Josiah Opina, Prekindergarten

# LET'S WRITE!

***Think about a time your plans changed.***

## Quick List

- Recess was held inside
- A restaurant was closed
- A trip got cancelled
- A store was closed
- It rained

## Text Structure

### Change of Plans

| We started to do this . . . | . . . because we were planning to do this . . . | But then we had to do this . . . | . . . because this happened. |
|---|---|---|---|

Polly, Put the Kettle On

## Kernel Essay

**My Kernel: Karina's was closed.**

1. We were driving to a restaurant . . .
2. . . . because we were hungry for their pancakes.
3. But we got there and had to figure out where else to go . . .
4. . . . because the restaurant was out of business.

## Bonus!

### Grammar and Spelling Connections

- repetition
- proper nouns
- contractions
- antonyms
- double consonants

**NURSERY RHYME**

## Polly, Put the Kettle On

**P**olly, put the kettle on, Polly, put the kettle on,

Polly, put the kettle on,

**W**e'll all have tea.

**S**ukey, take it off again, Sukey, take it off again,

Sukey, take it off again,

**T**hey've all gone away.

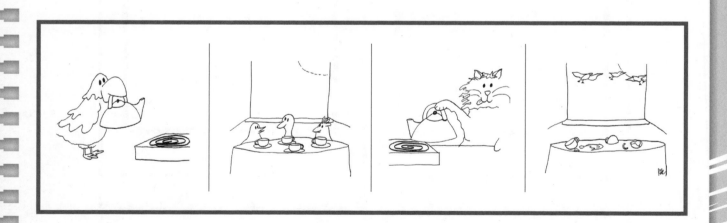

# STUDENT KERNEL
## Change of Plans

My Topic: Going to the playground

**1** We started to do this...

We started to go to the playground.

**2** ...Because we were planning to do this.

We were planning to swing on the swings.

**3** But then we had to do this...

Before we could swing we had to run into the shelter

**4** ...because this happened.

We had to run into the shelter because it started to rain.

Charleen Shook, Grandmother

# STUDENT KERNEL
## Change of Plans

Rory Shook, Kindergarten

**Think about a time you asked someone about something they did.**

**Quick List**

- Someone leaves the room and comes back
- Someone is absent
- Someone goes on a trip
- Someone goes to the nurse

**Text Structure**

### Small Talk

| Question: Where did you go? | Answer: I went . . . | Question: What did you do? | Answer: I . . . |

Pussycat, Pussycat

**Kernel Essay**

**My Kernel: Lilly**

1. Lilly, Lilly, where have you been?
2. I've been to the beach.
3. Lilly, Lilly, what did you do there?
4. I dug in the sand, swam in the waves, collected seashells, and flew a kite.

**Bonus!**

**Grammar and Spelling Connections**

- word order
- prepositions
- proper nouns
- double letters
- quotations
- three sentence types
- dialogue

## Pussycat, Pussycat

"**P**ussycat, pussycat, where have you been?"

"**I**'ve been up to London to visit the Queen."

"**P**ussycat, pussycat, what did you there?"

"**I** frightened a little mouse under her chair!"

# STUDENT KERNEL
## Small Talk

Leah, Leah where have you been?
"I've been to New Orleans to visit the aquarem" Leah, Leah, what did you there? "I learned about Sea animals."

Leah Staas, Grade 1

RYDER RYDER? Where have you Been? I've Been to New York to Visit My faMaliy RYDER RYDER? What did you there I tock a pecher av the Stachue of liBReti

Ryder Balmos, Grade 1

# STUDENT KERNEL
## Small Talk

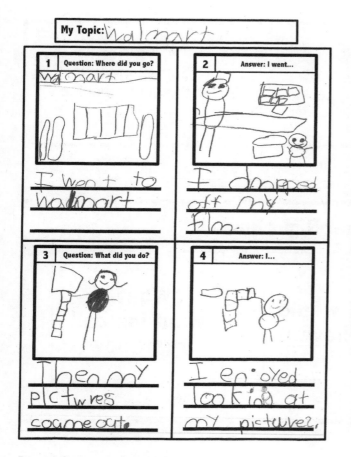

David Salazar, Grade 1

Samantha Inmon, Grade 2

# LET'S WRITE!

*Think about something you got at the wrong time and what you wanted instead.*

### Quick List

- A gift
- An activity
- Bedtime
- Sleep
- A prize
- Something from the gum machine

### Text Structure

**I Don't Want That Right Now**

| What I have | When I would rather have it | What I want instead right now |
|---|---|---|

Rain, Rain, Go Away

### Kernel Essay

**My Kernel: Bedtime**

1. It's bedtime.
2. I wish my bedtime were at midnight.
3. Right now I wish I could stay up and watch YouTube.

### Bonus!

**Grammar and Spelling Connections**

- long **a**
- commands
- personification
- double letters
- proper nouns
- write own name

# Rain, Rain, Go Away

**R**ain, rain, go away,

**C**ome again another day;

**L**ittle Johnny wants to play!

# STUDENT KERNEL
## I Don't Want That Right Now

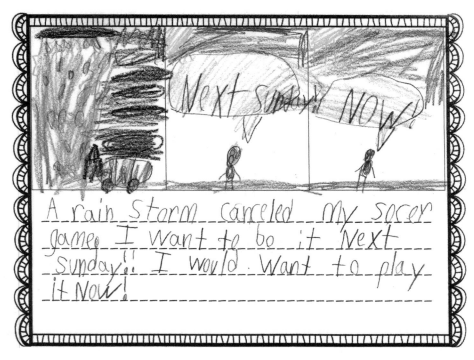

A rain storm canceled my socer game. I want to bo it Next sunday!! I would want to play it Now!

Jacob Stout, Grade 1

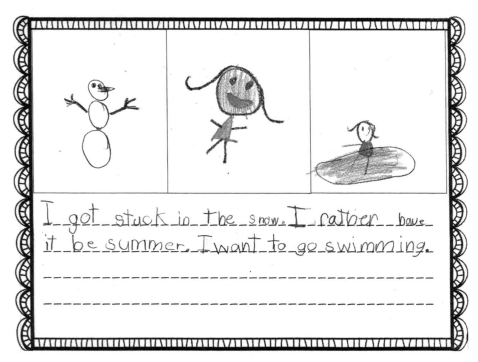

I got stuck in the snow. I rather have it be summer. I want to go swimming.

Jaime King, Grade 1

# STUDENT KERNEL
## I Don't Want That Right Now

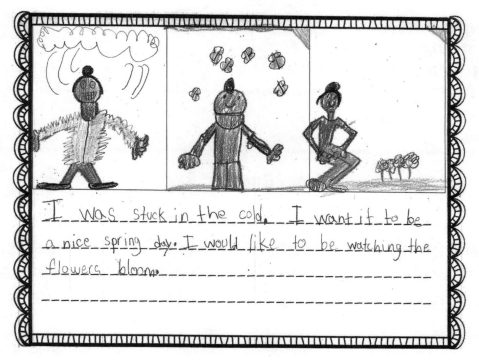

I was stuck in the cold. I want it to be a nice spring day. I would like to be watching the flowers bloom.

Zoe Hatcher, Grade 1

time

no traffic

NEVER

I was stuck in traffic for 4 hours. I never want it ever again. I want to Drive home with no traffic.

Zachary Thompson, Grade 1

# LET'S WRITE!

**Think about a time when something started out well but went very badly.**

**Quick List**

- A fall
- An injury
- A bad game
- A bad picnic

**Text Structure**

## From Good to Bad

| Something good was happening | Something began to go wrong | It went really wrong | It got even worse— very bad |

Rock-a-Bye Baby

**Kernel Essay**

**My Kernel: The Basketball Game**

1. My friend was playing basketball.
2. Our team started to lose.
3. Then they started getting mad.
4. At the end of the game, everyone on our team was unhappy.

**Bonus!**

**Grammar and Spelling Connections**

- **ock**
- AAAWWWUBIS (subordinating conjunctions like *after, although, as, while, when, wherever, until, because, if, since*)
- order of words
- **all**
- **le**
- double **l**
- present/future verbs
- short/long vowels

## Rock-a-Bye Baby

**R**ock-a-bye baby in the tree top,

**W**hen the wind blows, the cradle will rock.

**W**hen the bough breaks, the cradle will fall,

**A**nd down will come baby, cradle and all.

# STUDENT KERNEL
## From Good to Bad

**My Topic:** Babies can Give You Scarlet Fever

**1 Something good was happening**

I had a baby.

**2 Something began to go wrong**

It had a parasite.

**3 It went really wrong**

I touched it.

**4 It got even worse. Very bad.**

I got scarlet fever.

Dailyn Morgan, Grade 4

# STUDENT KERNEL
## From Good to Bad

**My Topic:** The Swing Broke (dictated to teacher)

**1 Something good was happening**

One day I was swinging at a park.

**2 Something began to go wrong**

The swing started to break.

**3 It went really wrong**

I got off as quickly as I can.

**4 It got even worse. Very bad.**

Then I got off by the time it fell.

Oliver Reimer, Prekindergarten

# LET'S WRITE!

**Think about new groups you might meet.**

**Quick List**

- New friends
- Cartoon characters
- New neighbors

**Text Structure**

## Who's That?

| Question: Who are they? | Answer: Who they are | What we should do with them |
|---|---|---|

Rub-a-Dub-Dub

**Kernel Essay**

**My Kernel: The New Family**

1. Who are those people walking their dog?
2. It's a new family in the neighborhood: Josh, Michelle, Sylvie, and the baby.
3. Let's make friends!

**Bonus!**

**Grammar and Spelling Connections**

- *cvc* (consonant-vowel-consonant) words
- alliteration
- compound words
- silent **k**
- commas in a series
- **er**
- long **e**

NURSERY RHYME

## Rub-a-Dub-Dub

**R**ub-a-dub-dub, three men in a tub,

And who do you think they be?

**T**he butcher, the baker, the candlestick-maker;

**T**urn them out, knaves all three!

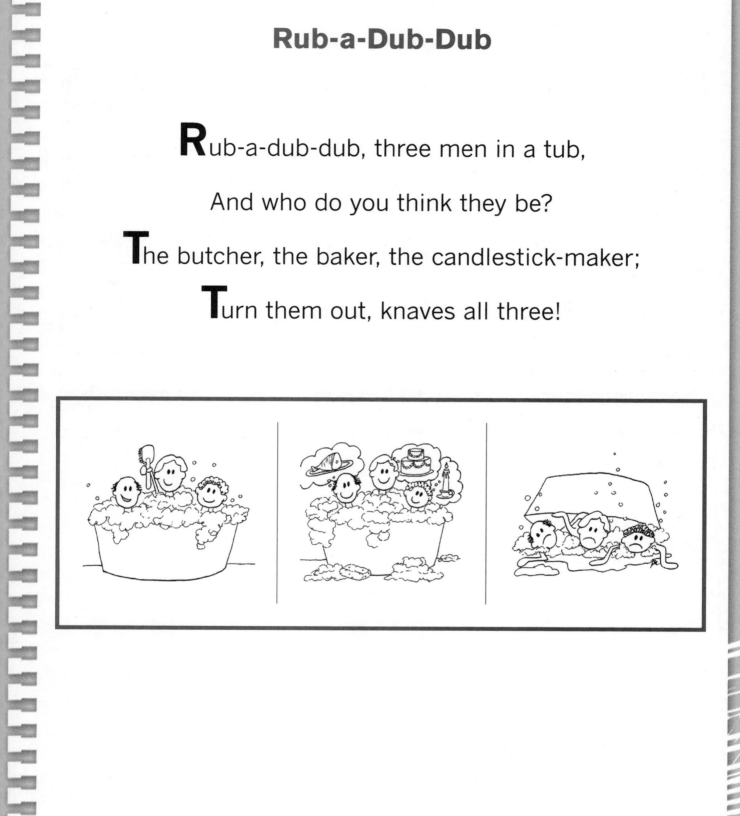

# STUDENT KERNEL
## Who's That?

**My Topic:** Crimals

| 1 — Q: Who are they? | 2 — A: Who they are | 3 — What we should do with them |
|---|---|---|
| Three crimonls | An avil crimal<br>A happy crimal<br>A confused crimal | Acrest them |

Dailyn Morgan, Grade 4

# STUDENT KERNEL

## Who's That?

**My Topic:** Friends

| 1 | Q: Who are they? | 2 | A: Who they are | 3 | What we should do with them |
|---|---|---|---|---|---|

Three friends.

Jacob, Dailyn, and Katie.

We should play with them!

Katelyn Luna, Grade 4

*Think about working for money in some kind of job.*

**Quick List**

- Classroom jobs
- Chores at home

**Text Structure**

### New Job

| Your job | What you will get for your work | Why you will get paid that |
|---|---|---|

Seesaw Margery Daw

**Kernel Essay**

**My Kernel: Allowance**

1. I have to earn my allowance.
2. Each week I get $3.00.
3. I will get more when I get older.

**Bonus!**

**Grammar and Spelling Connections**

- proper nouns
- names
- pronouns
- end in **y**
- contractions
- double letters
- **aw, au**

- AAAWWWUBIS (subordinating conjunctions like *after, although, as, while, when, wherever, until, because, if, since*)

## Seesaw Margery Daw

**S**eesaw Margery Daw

Johnny shall have a new master;

**H**e shall earn but a penny a day,

**B**ecause he can't work any faster.

# STUDENT KERNEL
## New Job

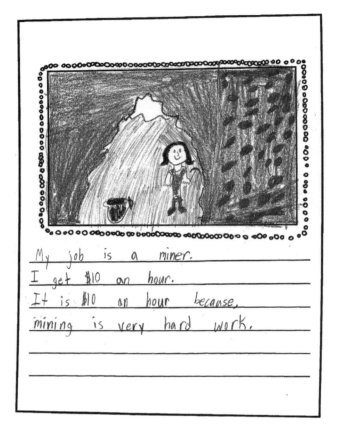

My job is a miner.
I get $10 an hour.
It is $10 an hour because,
mining is very hard work.

Mike Luna, Grade 4

When I was 12, I got a
job picking cucumbers. They paid
me 50¢ an hour. I was little
and couldn't carry a full bushel
basket, so I didn't make very
much.

Bert Shoopman, Author's Father

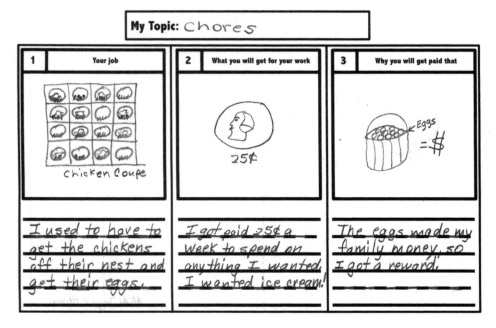

**My Topic:** Chores

| 1 | Your job | 2 | What you will get for your work | 3 | Why you will get paid that |
|---|---|---|---|---|---|

Chicken Coupe

25¢

Eggs
=$

I used to have to
get the chickens
off their nest and
get their eggs.

I got paid 25¢ a
week to spend on
anything I wanted.
I wanted ice cream!

The eggs made my
family money, so
I got a reward.

Samantha Inmon, Grade 2

# STUDENT KERNEL
## New Job

My job is working for Hephaestos. I only get half a penny. I get only half a penny because I only make a sword handle a day.

Ruby Morgan, Grade 4

**My Topic:** Cleaning Cody's Closet

| 1 Your job | 2 What you will get for your work | 3 Why you will get paid that |
| --- | --- | --- |
| For some reason, I decided to clean Cody's very messy closet. | I was very young, so I did all that cleaning for just ONE penny. | I got one penny because Cody, my brother, conned me into it! |

Jennifer Irvin, Mom and Teacher

# LET'S WRITE!

*Think about a time when someone asked you for something and you said no.*

**Quick List**

- Your lunch
- A toy
- Your pencil
- Your turn
- Your spot in line

**Text Structure**

## No, You Can't Have My Things—A Dialogue

| Two people see each other | What one of them asks for | The other person says no | The other person says okay |
|---|---|---|---|

Simple Simon

**Kernel Essay**

**My Kernel: The Glow-in-the-Dark Spinner**

1. Emma saw me.
2. She asked me if she could have my spinner.
3. I told her no.
4. She said okay.

**Bonus!**

**Grammar and Spelling Connections**

- alliteration
- dialogue
- title (*Sir*)
- order of words
- compound words
- common/proper nouns

## Simple Simon

**S**imple Simon met a pieman
going to the fair;

**S**aid Simple Simon to the pieman,
"Let me taste your ware."

**S**aid the pieman to Simple Simon,
"Show me first your penny."

**S**aid Simple Simon to the pieman,
"Sir, I have not any!"

# STUDENT KERNEL

## No, You Can't Have My Things—A Dialogue

Rory Shook, Kindergarten

# STUDENT KERNEL

## No, You Can't Have My Things—A Dialogue

My Topic: THE WAGON with Dick and Jane

**1 Two people see each other**

Dick and JANE meet in the PARK.

**2 What one of them asks for**

*May I Ride In your wagon?*

Dick ask Jane for A RIDE IN her wagon.

**3 The other person says no**

*No, I need to get Home.*

Jane tells Dick SHE'S unable to give Dick A RIDE because she needs to get home.

**4 The other person says okay**

*okay, see you tomorrow Jane.*

Dick says it's okay, that he will see Jane tomorrow.

Jerry Shook, Grandfather

# LET'S WRITE!

**Think about a time when something strange happened.**

### Quick List

- A raccoon got into your kitchen
- A skunk sprayed your dog
- Someone got unexpectedly sick

### Text Structure

**Something Crazy Happened**

| Something strange that happened | What one person was doing right then | What another person was doing right then | What another person was doing at that time |

Sing a Song of Sixpence

### Kernel Essay

**My Kernel: The Jellyfish Costumes**

1. The sun went down and the Halloween costumes lit up.
2. Kim looked like a tall jellyfish.
3. Julian looked like a short jellyfish.
4. Matilde looked like a slender jellyfish.

### Bonus!

**Grammar and Spelling Connections**

- vowel teams
- alliteration
- prepositions
- past/present
- **-ing**
- pitchforking (embedding lists in writing)
- number words

## Sing a Song of Sixpence

**S**ing a song of sixpence, a pocket full of rye,

Four and twenty blackbirds, baked in a pie.

When the pie was opened the birds began to sing,

Oh, wasn't that a dainty dish to set before the king?

**T**he king was in his counting house, counting out his money,

**T**he queen was in the parlor, eating bread and honey.

**T**he maid was in the garden, hanging out the clothes,

When down came a blackbird and pecked off her nose!

# STUDENT KERNEL
## Something Crazy Happened

**My Topic:** raining in the house

**1** Something strange that happened

It's raining in the house.

**2** What one person was doing right then

one person was playing games.

**3** What another person was doing right then

another was doing the dishes.

**4** What another person was doing at that time

I was yelling it's raining in my house.

Payton Hathaway, Grade 4

# STUDENT KERNEL
## Something Crazy Happened

Madison Deines, Grade 4

*Think about a fun word to put into a story.*

**Quick List**

- Funny
- Mean
- Tall
- Juicy

**Text Structure**

### Fun Word Story (Put the fun word somewhere in each box)

| There was a _____ person | One thing they did one day | Another thing they did that day | Another thing they did that day |
|---|---|---|---|

There Was a Crooked Man

**Kernel Essay**

**My Kernel: Sad**

1. There was a sad lady
2. And she drove a sad car.
3. She married a sad man.
4. And they had some sad children.

**Bonus!**

**Grammar and Spelling Connections**

- repetition
- adjectives
- **oo** words
- **ou**
- **ough, augh**

## There Was a Crooked Man

**T**here was a crooked man, and he walked
a crooked mile.

**H**e found a crooked sixpence upon a crooked stile.

**H**e bought a crooked cat, which caught
a crooked mouse,

**A**nd they all lived together in a little crooked house.

# STUDENT KERNEL

## Fun Word Story

**My Topic:** flopy Man

| | |
|---|---|
| **1** There was a _____ person | **2** One thing they did one day |
| There was a flopy man. | And hey dov a flopy car |
| **3** Another thing they did that day | **4** Another thing they did that day |
| and he Dove a flopy Bike. | and he had a flopy Pisle. |

Vincent Porras, Grade 2

# STUDENT KERNEL
## Fun Word Story

**My Topic:** FluFFy dog

**1** There was a _____ person

There was
a FluFFy dog.

**2** One thing they did one day

The FluFFy
dog walking
to The FluFFy shop.

**3** Another thing they did that day

She Sawe
a FluFFy cat.

**4** Another thing they did that day

She went to
The Dog Park
and She Sawe and
FluFFy Dog.

Jaydyn Gamez, Grade 2

# LET'S WRITE!

*Think about a problem you can't fix.*

## Quick List

- Closets too small
- Having to share rooms
- Socks that don't match
- Not having pencils
- Being thirsty

## Text Structure

### Problem That Can't Be Fixed

| Where I was | What I didn't have | What that made me do | What that made me do |

There Was an Old Woman

## Kernel Essay

**My Kernel: Too Much Homework**

1. I was at home.
2. I didn't have free time because I had too much homework to do.
3. That ruined another day.
4. It also made me never want to give kids homework if I'm ever a teacher.

## Bonus!

**Grammar and Spelling Connections**

- short/long vowels
- adverbs
- double consonants
- pronouns
- adjectives
- irregular nouns/plural
- digraphs **sh, wh**

# There Was an Old Woman

**T**here was an old woman who lived in a shoe.

**S**he had so many children she didn't know what to do!

**S**o she gave them some broth without any bread,

**A**nd she whipped them all soundly and sent them to bed!

# STUDENT KERNEL
## Problem That Can't Be Fixed

1. I was single for the first time in 20 years and had no idea how to date.

2. So I signed up for Tinder — an app designed to match potential candidates for dating by swiping "left" or "right".

3. We both swiped right, but after a few messages — nothing. We met serendipitously a month later and have been inseparable the last year and a half.

Colleen Narens, Teacher

One day it was my birthday oh I donst have UNUf JUdkas for everyone. I asked my mom for more JUdkas she said No. then I asked my sister she said No.

Julia Wright, Grade 1

# STUDENT KERNEL
## Problem That Can't Be Fixed

I was so tired sitting at home.
There was so much laundry, I couldn't keep up.
Bundles, and bundles around.
I hid in my room hoping I won't be found.

So much to do, so little time.
Laundry kept piling on the ground.
Bundles and bundles around.
I hid in my room hoping I wouldn't be found.

Jennifer Irvin, Mom and Teacher

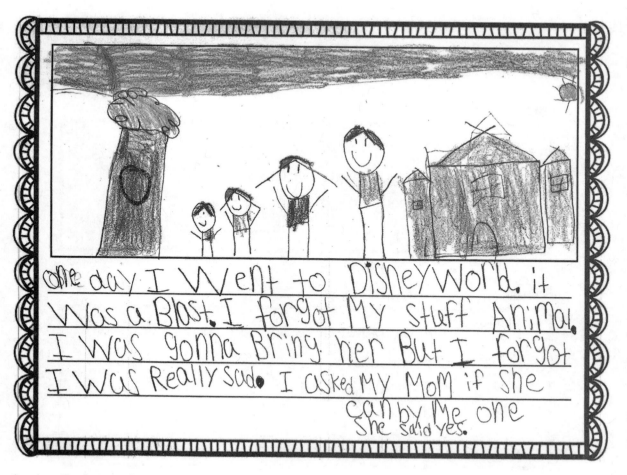

One day I went to Disney World. it was a Blast. I forgot My stuff Animal. I was gonna Bring her But I forgot I was Really sad. I asked My Mom if she can by Me one She said yes.

Jordan Redman, Grade 1

**Think about the last time you went to the store and what you bought there.**

**Quick List**

- Flip flops
- Sunglasses
- Toothpaste
- Toilet paper

**Text Structure**

## Going Shopping

| First I bought . . . | Then I bought . . . | Last I bought . . . |
|---|---|---|

To Market, to Market

**Kernel Essay**

**My Kernel: Hardware Store**

1. First I bought some ball bearings.
2. Then I bought a tiny flashlight.
3. Last I bought a wooden dowel.

**Bonus!**

**Grammar and Spelling Connections**

- *cvc* (consonant-vowel-consonant)
- words
- blends
- short vowels
- repetition
- **ar**

**NURSERY RHYME**

## To Market, to Market

To market, to market, to buy a fat pig;

Home again, home again, jiggety-jig.

To market, to market, to buy a fat hog;

Home again, home again, jiggety-jog.

To market, to market, to buy a plum bun;

Home again, home again, market is done.

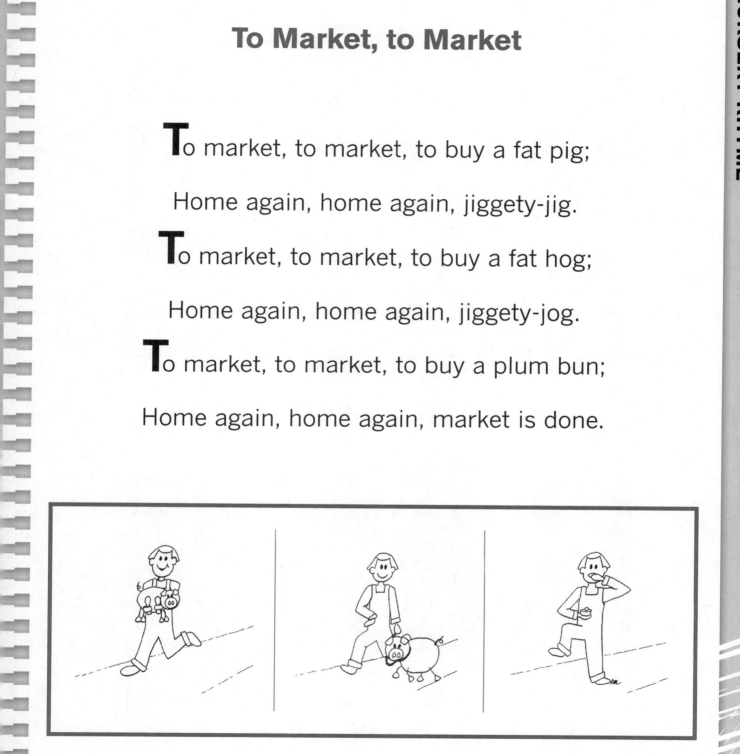

# STUDENT KERNEL
## Going Shopping

My Topic: luces

| 1 First I bought... | 2 Next I bought... | 3 Last I bought... |
|---|---|---|
| I got fures | Sageo IBHdHie | LasD Iga+ Spreos |

Jeriah Hernandez, Kindergarten

My Topic: corn dog

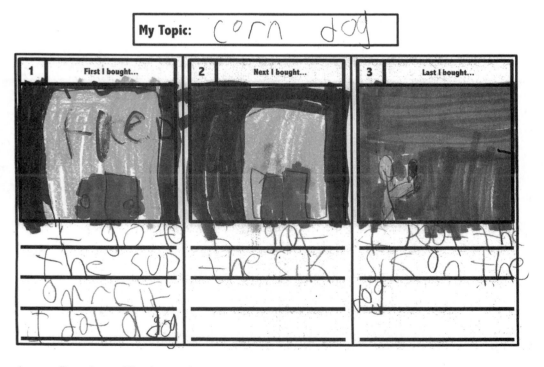

| 1 First I bought... | 2 Next I bought... | 3 Last I bought... |
|---|---|---|
| I go to the sup onrCif I dot a dog | I got the sik | I Rot the sik on the dog |

Jovan Ramirez, Kindergarten

# STUDENT KERNEL
## Going Shopping

**My Topic:** Spuaget

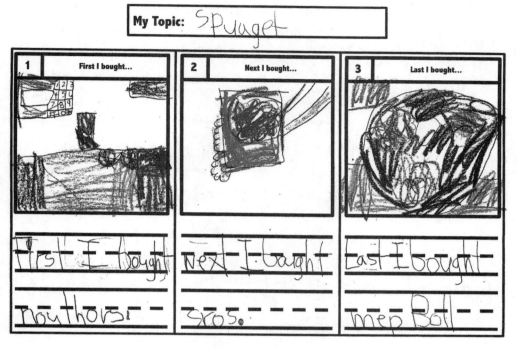

Victoria Hernandez, Kindergarten

**My Topic:** CUPCAKE

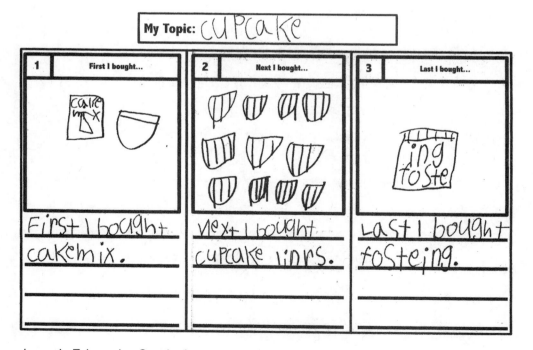

Joseph Edwards, Grade 1

# LET'S WRITE!

**Think about a time when someone broke a rule and what happened to them.**

**Quick List**

- Someone took someone else's toy
- Someone got out of line
- Someone took someone's pencil
- Someone ate someone else's food

**Text Structure**

## Somebody Broke a Rule

| Who did it | What they did | What happened to them |
|---|---|---|

Tom, Tom, the Piper's Son

**Kernel Essay**

**My Kernel: The Pushy Kid**

1. There was this kid on the playground.
2. He was acting like a bully.
3. The principal called him into her office and he cried and cried.

**Bonus!**

**Grammar and Spelling Connections**

- possessives
- prepositional phrases
- names in capital letters
- **st** blend
- long vowels

## Tom, Tom, the Piper's Son

**T**om, Tom, the piper's son,

**S**tole a pig and away did run.

**T**he pig was eat and Tom was beat

And Tom went crying down the street.

# STUDENT KERNEL
## Somebody Broke a Rule

I went to the zoo with my mom and dad. We saw a tiger and it ran away. We told the workers at the zoo that the tiger ran away.

Andy Garcia, Kindergarten

# STUDENT KERNEL
## Somebody Broke a Rule

When Billy, my friend, stole somthing from Dave and Busters, my dad caught him. He got punished.

Jose Ponce, Grade 3

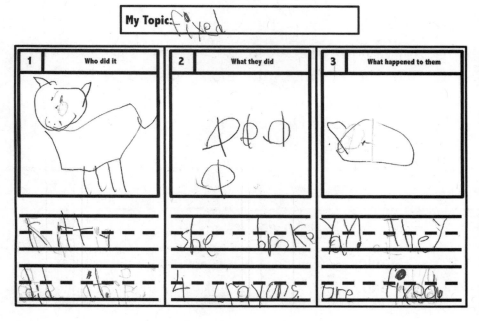

**My Topic:** fixed

| 1 | Who did it | 2 | What they did | 3 | What happened to them |
|---|---|---|---|---|---|

Kitty did this — she broke 4 crayons — yy they are fixed

Rory Shook, Kindergarten

# LET'S WRITE!

*Think about a time you fought with someone.*

## Quick List

- Fighting over who goes first
- Fighting over who sits in the front seat
- Fighting over who gets the first cupcake
- Fighting over friends

## Text Structure

### The Fight

| Who decided to fight | Why it started | What happened next | How the fight ended |
|---|---|---|---|

Tweedle-Dum and Tweedle-Dee

## Kernel Essay

**My Kernel: Playground Tussle**

1. A girl and a boy had a battle.
2. The girl had seen the boy throwing rocks at her friend.
3. She grabbed him by the shoulders and started kicking him.
4. Teachers peeled her off of him and they were both punished.

## Bonus!

**Grammar and Spelling Connections**

- similes
- blends
- **le**
- double consonants
- adjectives
- plural nouns

## Tweedle-Dum and Tweedle-Dee

Tweedle-Dum and Tweedle-Dee

Resolved to have a battle,

For Tweedle-Dum said Tweedle-Dee

Had spoiled his nice new rattle.

Just then flew by a monstrous crow,

As big as a tar-barrel,

Which frightened both the heroes so,

They quite forgot their battle.

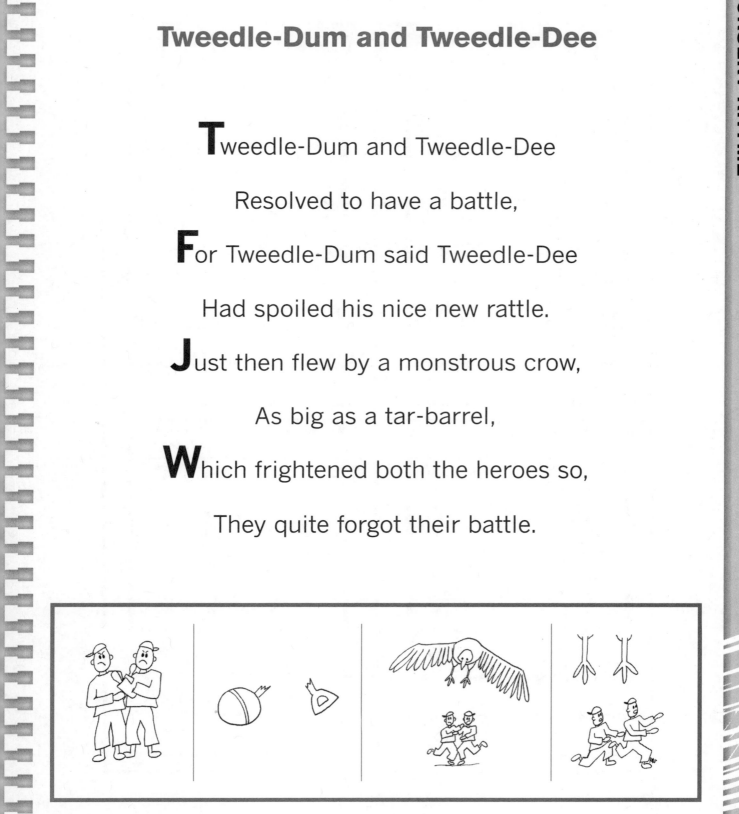

# STUDENT KERNEL
## The Fight

**My Topic:** Adianna scbra men

**1. Who decided to fight**

Adrianna was not his fa my,

**2. Why it started**

Adrianna scbr i wasx nis.

**3. What happened next**

criä and tnd Mrs. Rofrgiez

**4. How the fight ended**

Adrison got in cruble.

Nesarae Wolf, Grade 1

# STUDENT KERNEL
## The Fight

**My Topic:** My SISbr tast tays

| 1 | Who decided to fight |
|---|---|
| | |

Inoui wet My sesar

| 2 | Why it started |
|---|---|
| | |

My SeSer tuc my toy

| 3 | What happened next |
|---|---|
| | |

She cavit bac

| 4 | How the fight ended |
|---|---|
| | |

she beet racesr norters

Uziel Almanza, Grade 1

---

(dictated to teacher)

Quicklist:

* 1. Ariana and the toy dog
  2. Liam and the Power Ranger
  3. cookies
  4.

Kernel Essay:

1. Ariana wanted the toy dog that I was playing with.

2. She took it away from me.

3. We saw a scary shadow.

4. Then we stopped fighting and I let her take it.

Oliver Reimer, Kindergarten

*If something came to life, think about what you'd say to it.*

## Quick List

- Water bottle
- The rain
- A toy
- A hamburger
- A chair

## Text Structure

### Talking to Something—Personification

| What it is and the question | Where it is | What it looks like | What it is and the question |
|---|---|---|---|

Twinkle, Twinkle, Little Star

## Kernel Essay

**My Kernel: Blanket**

1. Blanket, blanket, what do you do when I'm not with you?
2. You stay snuggled there on my bed.
3. You're soft and blue, worn and happy.
4. Blanket, what do you do when you're not with me?

## Bonus!

**Grammar and Spelling Connections**

- similes
- prepositions
- commands
- **tw** blend
- **le**
- **er, ar**
- personification

## Twinkle, Twinkle, Little Star

**T**winkle, twinkle, little star,

How I wonder what you are.

**U**p above the world so high,

**L**ike a diamond in the sky.

**T**winkle, twinkle, little star,

How I wonder what you are.

# STUDENT KERNEL
## Talking to Something—Personification

**My Topic:** loine what are you

**1 What it is and the question**

Loine what do you mean when you rour!

**2 Where it is**

you are in a dark cove.

**3 What it is looks like**

you look like a sum flower

**4 What it is and the question**

Loine what do you mean whe you rour!

Adam Vega, Grade 2

# STUDENT KERNEL
## Talking to Something—Personification

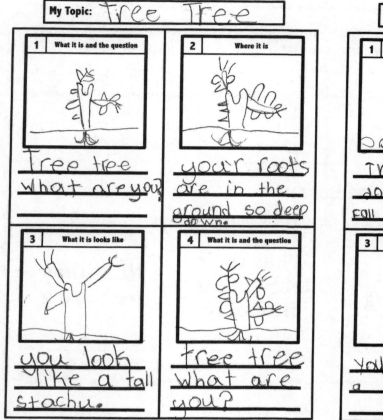

My Topic: Tree Tree

**1** What it is and the question

**2** Where it is

Tree tree
What are you

your roots
are in the
ground so deep
down.

**3** What it is looks like

**4** What it is and the question

you look
like a tall
stachu.

tree tree
what are
you?

Willow Spencer, Grade 2

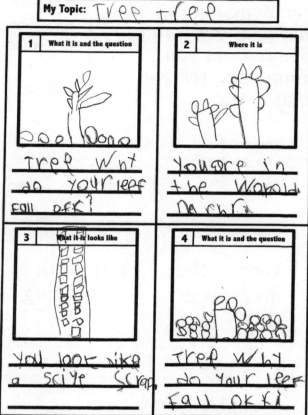

My Topic: Tree tree

**1** What it is and the question

**2** Where it is

Tree wht
do your leef
fall off?

You are in
the wohld
na chra

**3** What it is looks like

**4** What it is and the question

you look like
a sciye scrap.

Tree why
do your leef
fall off!

Tristan Berthold, Grade 1

*Think of someone (someone not in charge of you) who tries to boss you around and tell you what to do.*

### Quick List

- Friends telling you which friends you can have
- Other students telling you what to do
- Your sisters/brothers

### Text Structure

**Too Bossy**

| Where the person is | Where they are going | What their feet/hands are doing | What they are saying |

Wee Willie Winkie

### Kernel Essay

**My Kernel: Onnie and the Seagulls**

1. Onnie was on the beach.
2. She ran over to where a family was feeding the seagulls.
3. She was waving her arms and shouting at them.
4. "You're not supposed to give them chips! It's bad for them!"

### Bonus!

**Grammar and Spelling Connections**

- alliteration
- compound words
- **ck**
- **ow**
- "their"
- dialogue
- opposites
- irregular plurals
- prepositions
- fanboys (coordinating conjunctions: *for, and, nor, but, or, yet, so*)

## Wee Willie Winkie

**W**ee Willie Winkie runs through the town,

**U**pstairs and downstairs in his nightgown,

**T**apping at the window and crying through the lock,

**"A**re the children in their bed, for now it's ten o'clock?"

# STUDENT KERNEL
## Too Bossy

**My Topic:** John Cena wrestling.

| 1 Where the person is | 2 Where they are going |
|---|---|

John Cena is in the stadium.

John Cena is going to the wrestling ring

| 3 What their feet/hands are doing | 4 What they were saying |
|---|---|

And his name is John Cena.

He is bodyslamming someone.

"And his name is John Cena!

Alex Avalos, Grade 4

# STUDENT KERNEL
## Too Bossy

**My Topic:** Dailyn

| 1 | Where the person is |
|---|---|

Dailyn is in bed.

| 2 | Where they are going |
|---|---|

She is going to sleep.

| 3 | What their feet/hands are doing |
|---|---|

Her hands are wiggling.

| 4 | What they were saying |
|---|---|

She was saying what is in her dreams.

Katelyn Luna, Grade 4

# Appendices

# Appendix 1

## Complete Collection of 53 Text Structures

### Not What I Thought Would Happen

| How surprised I am | What you used to do | What you do now |

A Diller, a Dollar

### Something I Used to Have

| What I used to have | What happened to it | How it ended |

Betty Pringle

### Spotting Someone Famous

| Where I was | Who I saw | What I thought |

As I Was Going by Charing Cross

### Someone Left

| Somebody went away | What they looked like | What I want them to do |

Bobby Shaftoe

### More Than One

| Question: Do you have _____ ? | Answer: Yes, I have _____ . | List them. |

Baa, Baa, Black Sheep

### Big News!

| You'll never believe this. | I've got news! | You'll never believe this. | The news is . . . |

Brave News Is Come to Town

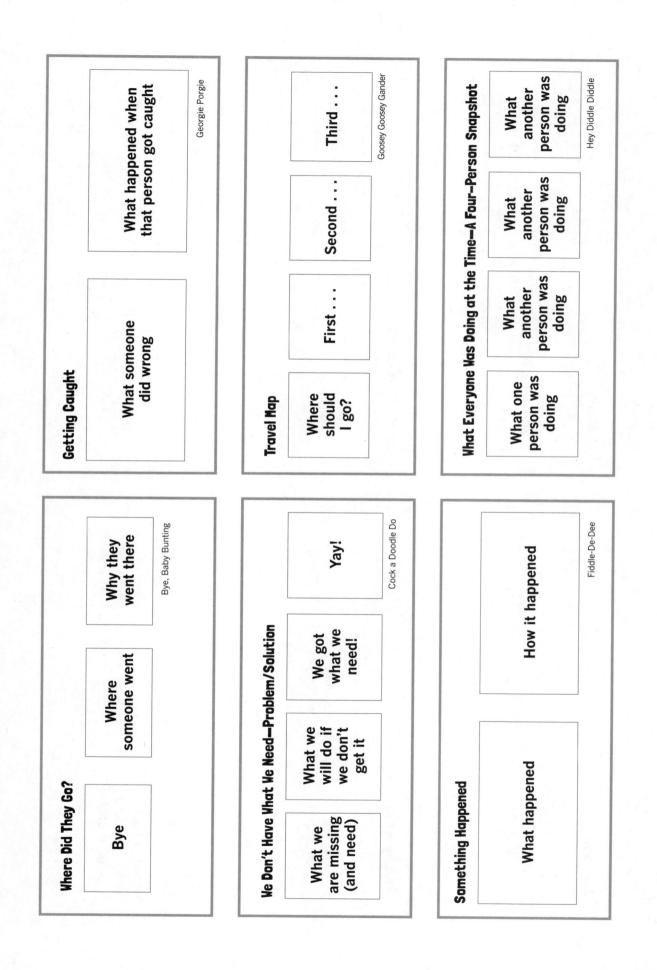

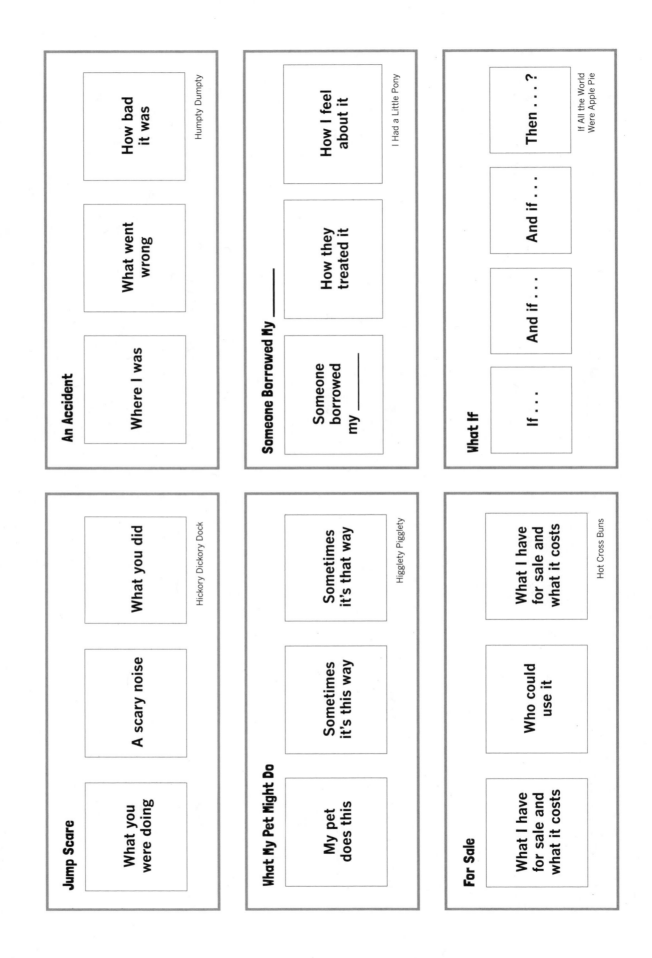

**An Accident**

| Where I was | What went wrong | How bad it was |
|---|---|---|

Humpty Dumpty

**Someone Borrowed My ___**

| Someone borrowed my ___ | How they treated it | How I feel about it |
|---|---|---|

I Had a Little Pony

**What If**

| If . . . | And if . . . | And if . . . | Then . . . ? |
|---|---|---|---|

If All the World Were Apple Pie

**Jump Scare**

| What you were doing | A scary noise | What you did |
|---|---|---|

Hickory Dickory Dock

**What My Pet Might Do**

| My pet does this | Sometimes it's this way | Sometimes it's that way |
|---|---|---|

Higglety Pigglety

**For Sale**

| What I have for sale and what it costs | Who could use it | What I have for sale and what it costs |
|---|---|---|

Hot Cross Buns

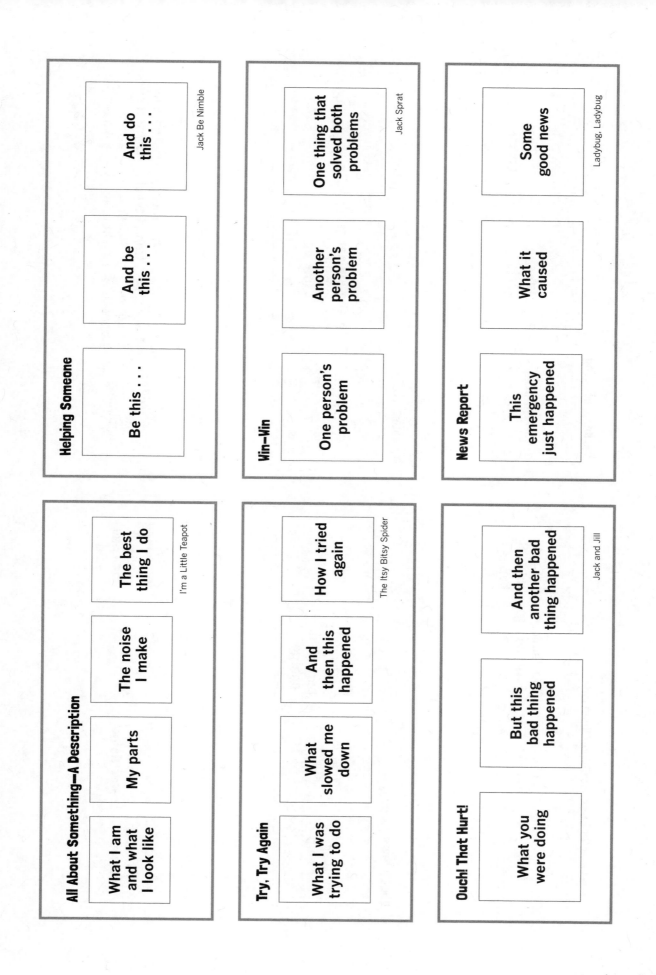

## Helping Someone

| Be this . . . | And be this . . . | And do this . . . |

Jack Be Nimble

## Win–Win

| One person's problem | Another person's problem | One thing that solved both problems |

Jack Sprat

## News Report

| This emergency just happened | What it caused | Some good news |

Ladybug, Ladybug

## All About Something—A Description

| What I am and what I look like | My parts | The noise I make | The best thing I do |

I'm a Little Teapot

## Try, Try Again

| What I was trying to do | What slowed me down | And then this happened | How I tried again |

The Itsy Bitsy Spider

## Ouch! That Hurt!

| What you were doing | But this bad thing happened | And then another bad thing happened |

Jack and Jill

## Defining a Feeling

| My name is . . . | When I feel . . . | That means . . . |
|---|---|---|

Little Jumping Joan

## My Short Story

| What you were doing | But suddenly a problem came up | What you did about it |
|---|---|---|

Little Miss Muffet

## Three Questions

| Someone did something | One thing I want to know about it | Another thing I want to know about it | And one more thing I want to know |
|---|---|---|---|

Little Tommy Tucker

## Something Is Lost—Problem/Solution

| I lost ___ | That means I can't ___ | So I think I will do this . . . | . . . and this will happen. |
|---|---|---|---|

Little Bo Peep

## What a Mess! Help!

| A call for help | What is going wrong | Question: Where's the person in charge? | Answer: That person is . . . |
|---|---|---|---|

Little Boy Blue

## Good Job!

| Where I was | What I was doing | What I did | Something nice someone said |
|---|---|---|---|

Little Jack Horner

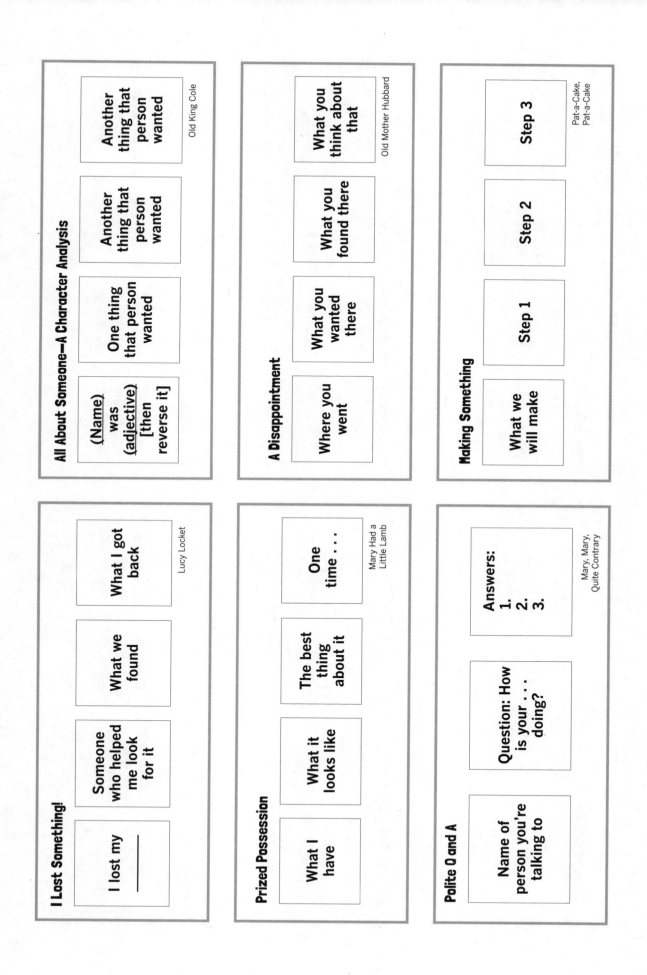

## All About Someone—A Character Analysis

| (Name) was (adjective) [then reverse it] | One thing that person wanted | Another thing that person wanted | Another thing that person wanted |

Old King Cole

## A Disappointment

| Where you went | What you wanted there | What you found there | What you think about that |

Old Mother Hubbard

## Making Something

| What we will make | Step 1 | Step 2 | Step 3 |

Pat-a-Cake, Pat-a-Cake

## I Lost Something!

| I lost my _____ | Someone who helped me look for it | What we found | What I got back |

Lucy Locket

## Prized Possession

| What I have | What it looks like | The best thing about it | One time . . . |

Mary Had a Little Lamb

## Polite Q and A

| Name of person you're talking to | Question: How is your . . . doing? | Answers: 1. 2. 3. |

Mary, Mary, Quite Contrary

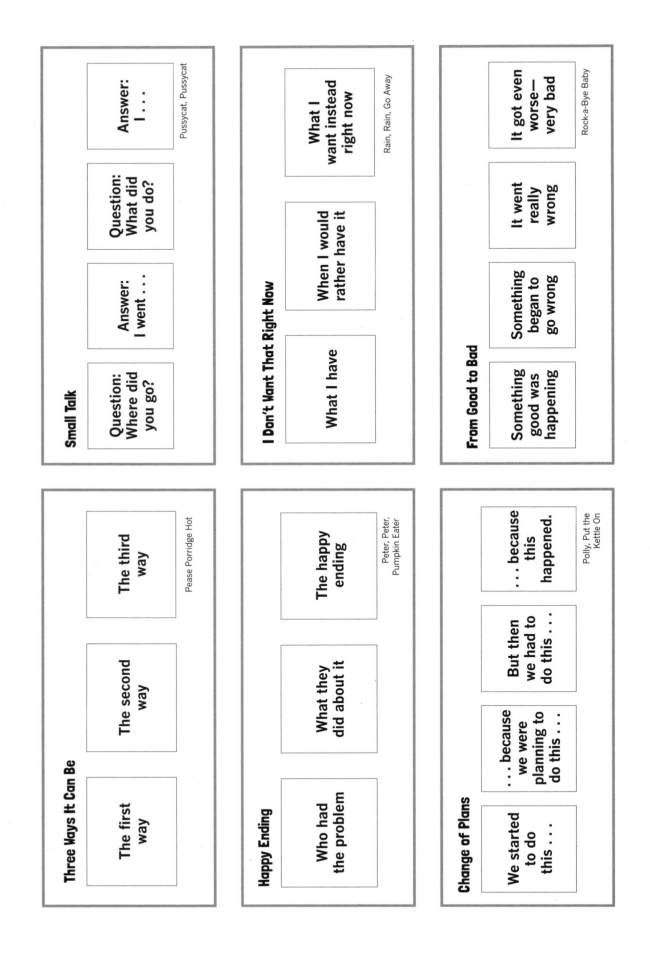

**Small Talk**

| Question: Where did you go? | Answer: I went . . . | Question: What did you do? | Answer: I . . . |

Pussycat, Pussycat

**I Don't Want That Right Now**

| What I have | When I would rather have it | What I want instead right now |

Rain, Rain, Go Away

**From Good to Bad**

| Something good was happening | Something began to go wrong | It went really wrong | It got even worse— very bad |

Rock-a-Bye Baby

**Three Ways It Can Be**

| The first way | The second way | The third way |

Pease Porridge Hot

**Happy Ending**

| Who had the problem | What they did about it | The happy ending |

Peter, Peter, Pumpkin Eater

**Change of Plans**

| We started to do this . . . | . . . because we were planning to do this . . . | But then we had to do this . . . | . . . because this happened. |

Polly, Put the Kettle On

## Something Crazy Happened

| Something strange that happened | What one person was doing right then | What another person was doing right then | What another person was doing at that time |
|---|---|---|---|

Sing a Song of Sixpence

## Fun Word Story (Put the fun word somewhere in each box)

| There was a _____ person | One thing they did one day | Another thing they did that day | Another thing they did that day |
|---|---|---|---|

There Was a Crooked Man

## Problem That Can't Be Fixed

| Where I was | What I didn't have | What that made me do |
|---|---|---|

There Was an Old Woman

## Who's That?

| Question: Who are they? | Answer: Who they are | What we should do with them |
|---|---|---|

Rub-a-Dub-Dub

## New Job

| Your job | What you will get for your work | Why you will get paid that |
|---|---|---|

Seesaw Margery Daw

## No, You Can't Have My Things—A Dialogue

| Two people see each other | What one of them asks for | The other person says no | The other person says okay |
|---|---|---|---|

Simple Simon

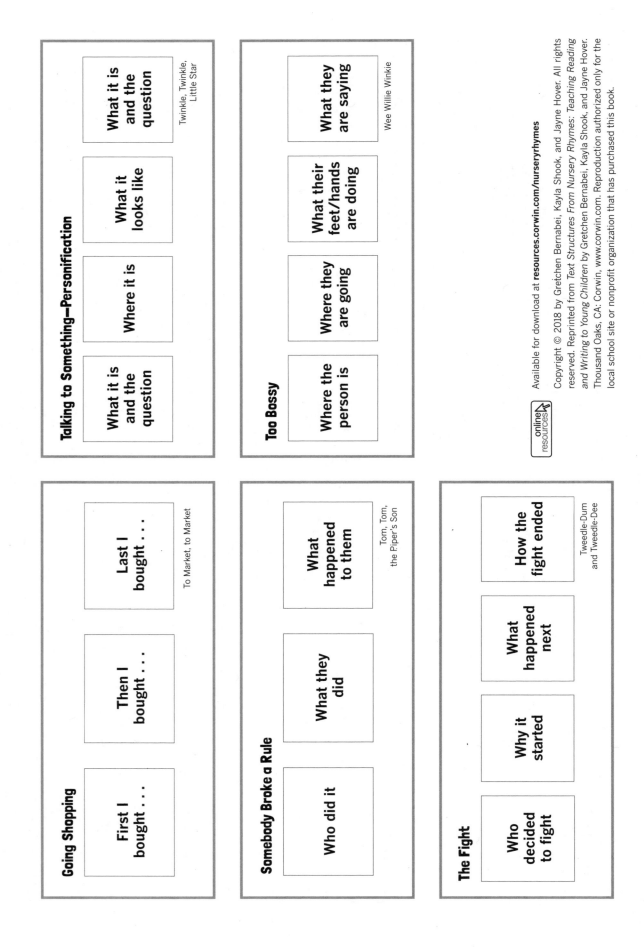

## Talking to Something—Personification

| What it is and the question | Where it is | What it looks like | What it is and the question |
| --- | --- | --- | --- |

Twinkle, Twinkle, Little Star

## Too Bossy

| Where the person is | Where they are going | What their feet/hands are doing | What they are saying |
| --- | --- | --- | --- |

Wee Willie Winkie

## Going Shopping

| First I bought . . . | Then I bought . . . | Last I bought . . . |
| --- | --- | --- |

To Market, to Market

## Somebody Broke a Rule

| Who did it | What they did | What happened to them |
| --- | --- | --- |

Tom, Tom, the Piper's Son

## The Fight

| Who decided to fight | Why it started | What happened next | How the fight ended |
| --- | --- | --- | --- |

Tweedle-Dum and Tweedle-Dee

# Appendix 2

## Text Structures for a Busy Town

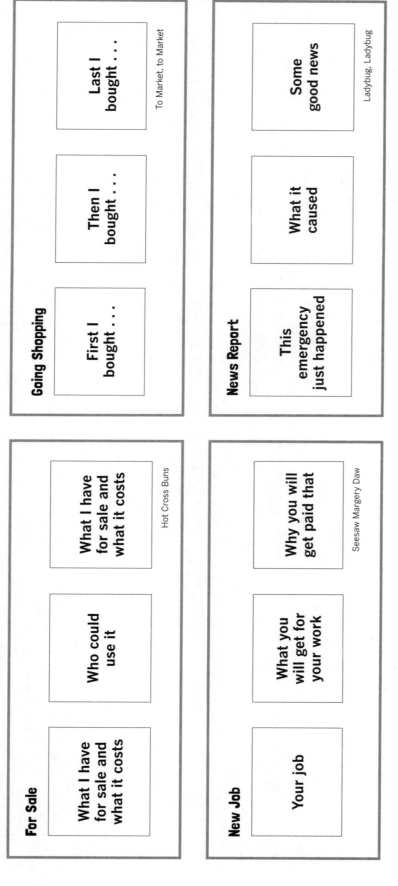

**Going Shopping**

| First I bought . . . | Then I bought . . . | Last I bought . . . |

To Market, to Market

**News Report**

| This emergency just happened | What it caused | Some good news |

Ladybug, Ladybug

**For Sale**

| What I have for sale and what it costs | Who could use it | What I have for sale and what it costs |

Hot Cross Buns

**New Job**

| Your job | What you will get for your work | Why you will get paid that |

Seesaw Margery Daw

online resources

Available for download at **resources.corwin.com/nurseryrhymes**

# Appendix 3

## Text Structures for Caring About Others

### Helping Someone

| Be this . . . | And be this . . . | And do this . . . |
|---|---|---|

Jack Be Nimble

### Three Questions

| Someone did something | One thing I want to know about it | Another thing I want to know about it | And one more thing I want to know |
|---|---|---|---|

Little Tommy Tucker

### Going Shopping

| First I bought . . . | Then I bought . . . | Last I bought . . . |
|---|---|---|

To Market, to Market

### What My Pet Might Do

| My pet does this | Sometimes it's this way | Sometimes it's that way |
|---|---|---|

Higglety Pigglety

### Something I Used to Have

| What I used to have | What happened to it | How it ended |
|---|---|---|

Betty Pringle

# Appendix 4

## Text Structures for Feelings

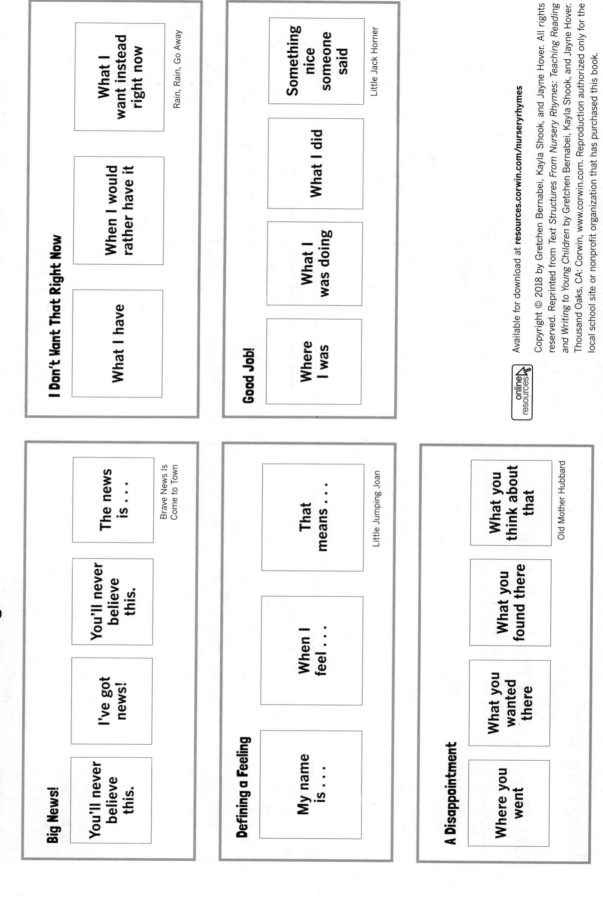

**Big News!**

You'll never believe this. | I've got news! | You'll never believe this. | The news is . . .

Brave News Is Come to Town

**Defining a Feeling**

My name is . . . | When I feel . . . | That means . . .

Little Jumping Joan

**A Disappointment**

Where you went | What you wanted there | What you found there | What you think about that

Old Mother Hubbard

**I Don't Want That Right Now**

What I have | When I would rather have it | What I want instead right now

Rain, Rain, Go Away

**Good Job!**

Where I was | What I was doing | What I did | Something nice someone said

Little Jack Horner

# Appendix 5

## Text Structures for Problem Solving

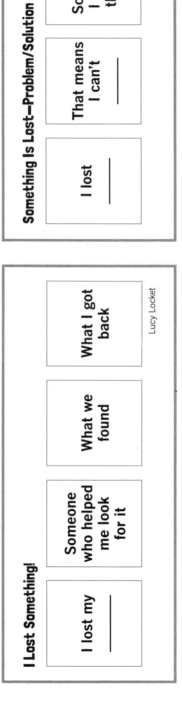

**I Lost Something!**

I lost my ___ | Someone who helped me look for it | What I got back

Lucy Locket

**Win–Win**

One person's problem | Another person's problem | One thing that solved both problems

Jack Sprat

**We Don't Have What We Need—Problem/Solution**

What we are missing (and need) | What we will do if we don't get it | We got what we need! | Yay!

Cock a Doodle Do

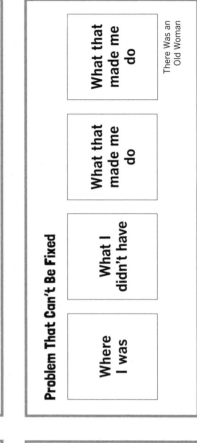

**Something Is Lost—Problem/Solution**

I lost ___ | That means I can't ___ | So I think I will do this . . . | . . . and this will happen.

Little Bo Peep

**Problem That Can't Be Fixed**

Where I was | What I didn't have | What that made me do | What that made me do

There Was an Old Woman

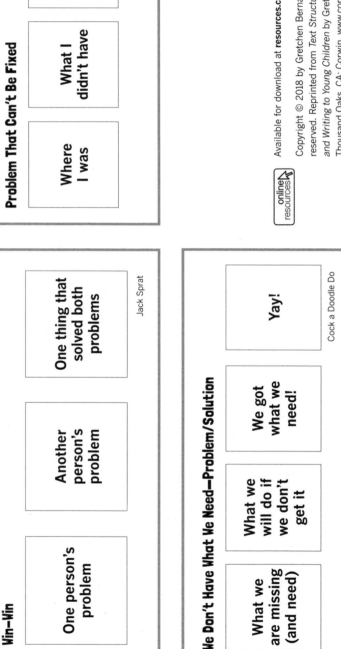

# Appendix 6

## Text Structures for Travel

**Where Did They Go?**

| Bye | Where someone went | Why they went there |
|---|---|---|

*Bye, Baby Bunting*

**Spotting Someone Famous**

| Where I was | Who I saw | What I thought |
|---|---|---|

*As I Was Going by Charing Cross*

**Someone Left**

| Somebody went away | What they looked like | What I want them to do |
|---|---|---|

*Bobby Shaftoe*

**Small Talk**

| Question: Where did you go? | Answer: I went . . . | Question: What did you do? | Answer: I . . . |
|---|---|---|---|

*Pussycat, Pussycat*

**Travel Map**

| Where should I go? | First . . . | Second . . . | Third . . . |
|---|---|---|---|

*Goosey Goosey Gander*

# Appendix 7

## Text Structures for Unfairness

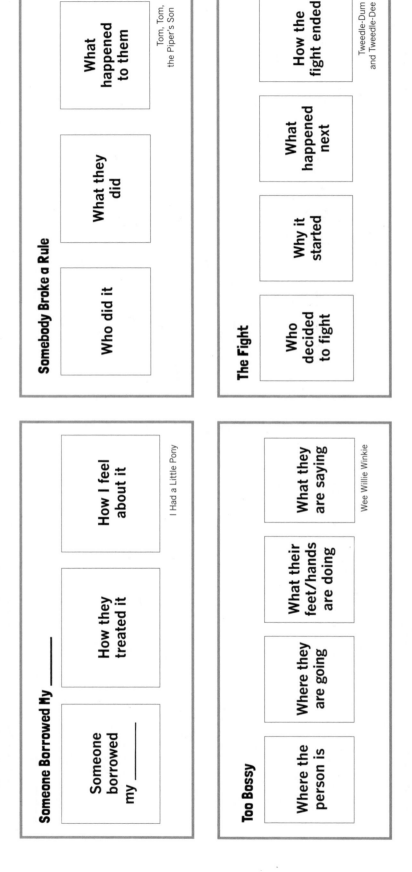

**Someone Borrowed My _____**

| Someone borrowed my _____ | How they treated it | How I feel about it |

I Had a Little Pony

**Somebody Broke a Rule**

| Who did it | What they did | What happened to them |

Tom, Tom, the Piper's Son

**Too Bossy**

| Where the person is | Where they are going | What their feet/hands are doing | What they are saying |

Wee Willie Winkie

**The Fight**

| Who decided to fight | Why it started | What happened next | How the fight ended |

Tweedle-Dum and Tweedle-Dee

online resources

Available for download at **resources.corwin.com/nurseryrhymes**

# Appendix 8

## Text Structures Just for Fun

### What If

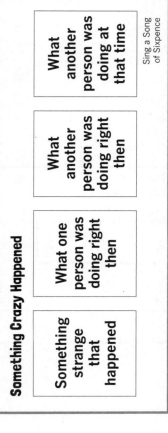

| If . . . | And if . . . | And if . . . | Then . . . ? |

*If All the World Were Apple Pie*

### Something Crazy Happened

| Something strange that happened | What one person was doing right then | What another person was doing right then | What another person was doing at that time |

*Sing a Song of Sixpence*

### Fun Word Story (Put the fun word somewhere in each box)

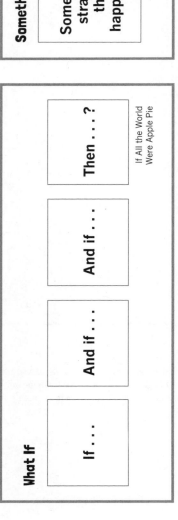

| There was a ___ person | One thing they did one day | Another thing they did that day | Another thing they did that day |

*There Was a Crooked Man*

### What Everyone Was Doing at the Time—A Four-Person Snapshot

| What one person was doing | What another person was doing | What another person was doing | What another person was doing |

*Hey Diddle Diddle*

online resources

# Appendix 9

## Text Structure Templates

**Name** _____ **Date** _____

| My Topic: |
|-----------|

### Text Structure:

| 1 | |
|---|--|
| | |

| 2 | |
|---|--|
| | |

**Name** _____ **Date** _____

My Topic:

## Text Structure:

| 1 | | 2 | |
|---|---|---|---|

**Name** _____ **Date** _____

My Topic:

## Text Structure:

| 1 | | 2 | |
|---|---|---|---|

_____

_____

_____

**Name** ———————————————————————————————— **Date** ——————————————

| My Topic: |
|---|

**Text Structure:**

| 1 | | 2 | | 3 | |
|---|---|---|---|---|---|
| | | | | | |

**Name** —————————————————————————— **Date** ——————————

My Topic: 

**Text Structure:**

| 1 | | 2 | | 3 | |
|---|---|---|---|---|---|

Name ______________________________ Date ______________

**My Topic:**

**Text Structure:**

| 1 | 2 | 3 |
| --- | --- | --- |
| | | |

online resources

Available for download at **resources.corwin.com/nurseryrhymes**

**Name:** _____

**My Topic:** _____

## Text Structure:

| 1 | |
|---|---|
| | |

_____

_____

_____

| 2 | |
|---|---|
| | |

_____

_____

_____

| 3 | |
|---|---|
| | |

_____

_____

_____

| 4 | |
|---|---|
| | |

_____

_____

_____

Available for download at **resources.corwin.com/nurseryrhymes**

**Name:** _____

**My Topic:** _____

**Text Structure:** _____

| 1 | | 2 | |
|---|---|---|---|

| 3 | | 4 | |
|---|---|---|---|

**Name:** _____

| **My Topic:** |
| :--- |

**Text Structure:**

# Appendix 10

## Stationery Templates

Name _____ Grade _____

Name _____ Grade ____

Name _____ Grade _____

_____

_____

_____

_____

_____

_____

Appendix 10   243

Name _____ Grade ____

_____

_____

_____

_____

_____

Name _____ Grade _____

_____

_____

_____

_____

_____

Name _____ Grade ____

_____

_____

_____

_____

_____

Name _____ Grade _____

_____

_____

_____

_____

_____

 Available for download at **resources.corwin.com/nurseryrhymes**

Name _____ Grade ____

<br>

```
┌─────────────────────────────────────────┐
│                                         │
│                                         │
│                                         │
│                                         │
│                                         │
│                                         │
│                                         │
│                                         │
│                                         │
│                                         │
│                                         │
│                                         │
│                                         │
└─────────────────────────────────────────┘
```

_____

_____

_____

_____

_____

# About the Authors

A popular workshop presenter and winner of NCTE's James Moffett Award in 2010, **Gretchen Bernabei** has been teaching kids to write in middle school and high school classrooms for more than thirty years. In addition to writing four other professional books and numerous articles for NCTE journals, she is the author of National Geographic School Publications' *The Good Writer's Kit*, as well as *Lightning in a Bottle*, a CD of visual writing prompts.

**Kayla Shook**, also known as Texas Teaching Fanatic, has been teaching fourth grade for nine years in central Texas. She works with teachers throughout the state to implement successful writing strategies. She lives with her husband and son in New Braunfels, Texas.

With more than thirty years in education, **Jayne Hover** has taught elementary, middle, and high school and has been an administrator in several roles from assistant principal to coaching teachers. Currently, she is in an administrative role with San Antonio ISD. Jayne is also a co-author of *Crunchtime* (2009, Heinemann). She lives near San Antonio, Texas, with her husband, Jim.

*hoverjayne@g*

*trails of bread crumbs*

# CORWIN LITERACY

### Wiley Blevins

Wiley Blevins explains the 7 ingredients that lead to the greatest student gains. Includes common pitfalls, lessons, word lists, and routines.

### Gravity Goldberg

Let go of the default roles of assigner, monitor, and manager, and shift to a growth mindset. The 4 *Ms* framework lightens your load by allowing students to monitor and direct their own reading lives.

### Nancy Frey, Douglas Fisher

Nancy Frey and Douglas Fisher articulate an instructional plan for close reading so clearly, and so squarely built on research, that it's the only resource a teacher will need.

### Nancy Boyles

20 close reading, standards-based lessons and 80 follow-up comprehension skill lessons expertly scaffold young readers. The lessons include day-to-day how to's, formative assessment, and performance criteria.

### Douglas Fisher, Nancy Frey, Heather Anderson, Marisol Thayre

Learn the best ways to use text-dependent questions as scaffolds during close reading and the big understandings they yield. Includes illustrative video, texts and questions, cross-curricular examples, and online facilitator's guides.

### Michael Rafferty, Colleen Morello, Paraskevi Rountos

This amazing 4-part framework—Engage, Discuss, Deep-See Think, and Connect—gets students interacting with texts, developing their literal, inferential, evaluative, and analytical skills.

# BECAUSE ALL TEACHERS ARE LEADERS

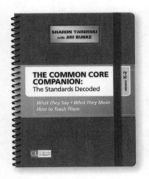

**Sharon Taberski, Jim Burke**

What makes *The Common Core Companion* "that version of the standards you wish you had"? The way it translates each and every standard into the day-to-day "what you do."

**Gretchen Bernabei, Judi Reimer**

If ever there were a book to increase students' test scores, this is it. Its 101 student essays and one-page lessons deliver powerhouse instruction on writing well in any genre.

**Sharon Taberski, Jim Burke**

This new version of *The Common Core Companion* provides indexes for states implementing state-specific ELA standards, allowing you to tap into the potency of standards-based teaching ideas.

**Gretchen Bernabei**

This kid-friendly cache of 101 lessons and practice pages helps your students internalize the conventions of correctness once and for all.

Corwin educator discount
★★★
**20% OFF EVERY DAY!**
★★★

800-233-9936

CL CORWIN LITERACY

N17857

A SAGE Publishing Company

**Helping educators make the greatest impact**

**CORWIN HAS ONE MISSION:** to enhance education through intentional professional learning.

We build long-term relationships with our authors, educators, clients, and associations who partner with us to develop and continuously improve the best evidence-based practices that establish and support lifelong learning.